The Freedom to Love

The Freedom to Love

*Recovery
and the
Seven
Deadly Sins*

Emmerich Vogt, O.P.

Mill City Press
Minneapolis, MN

Mill City Press, Inc.

212 3ʳᵈ Avenue North, Suite 290

Minneapolis, MN 55401

612.455.2294

www.millcitypublishing.com

ISBN-13: 978-1-938223-07-5

LCCN: 2012935385

Cover Design and Typeset by Sophie Chi

Printed in the United States of America

Nihil Obstat
Very Rev. Basil Burr Cole, OP, STD
Censor Deputatus
Imprimi Potest
Very Rev. Mark Christopher Padrez, OP
Prior Provincial
March 2012

To love at all is to be vulnerable. Love anything and your heart will be wrung and possibly broken. If you want to make sure of keeping it intact you must give it to no one, not even an animal. Wrap it carefully round with hobbies and little luxuries; avoid all entanglements. Lock it up safe in the casket or coffin of your selfishness. But in that casket, safe, dark, motionless, airless, it will change. It will not be broken; it will become unbreakable, impenetrable, irredeemable. To love is to be vulnerable.

—C.S. Lewis, *The Four Loves*

Dedication

> *There is nothing on this earth more to*
> *be prized than true friendship.*
>
> —St. Thomas Aquinas

It is only in and through the help and inspiration of friends
that the human heart is able to carry through with its dreams,
and such has been the case in my own life and ministry. After
some years in studying and living the principles of the twelve
steps and seeking to understand them in the full context of
Gospel living, I am able to present this small book. These
years of ministry in twelve-step spirituality would not have
been possible without the help of dear and supportive friends.
Most especially, the friendship and support of Bill and Michele
Maitland made it possible for me to carry on my twelve-step
ministry these last several years. I remain deeply grateful for
their untold support. My ministry, sharing the message of the
twelve steps in the context of Gospel principles, would not
have been possible without the voluntary and faithful help of
my dear friends Monica and Jim Glavin, who tirelessly run

the twelve-step ministry site. With the aid of Calvin Smith, Lauriette Hoover, Julie Klum, Pat Nuszbaum, Athena Drakos-Williams, and Maria-the-Peach, the Glavins have seen to the running of our little office and the publication and distribution of our CDs, DVDs, and pamphlets. A special note of gratitude should be made to Antoinette Doyle, a fellow Dominican, who thirty years ago encouraged me to learn the steps. My gratitude also extends to my Dominican brother, Fr. Basil Cole, for taking the time to read the manuscript and offer helpful comments and corrections. I owe a debt of gratitude to all these dear friends.

Table of Contents

Introduction

> *Two things are required in order to obtain eternal life: the grace of God and man's will. And although God made man without man's help, He does not sanctify him without his cooperation.*
>
> —St. Thomas Aquinas

Although I offer this book for those Christians involved in twelve-step recovery, I do not discuss "recovery" in the restricted sense of recovery as found in twelve-step programs purely and simply, but rather in the wider and Christian sense of recovery from the effects of sin in our lives, both original sin (i.e., the hereditary wound we have all received) and personal sin. Truly this is what recovery for the Christian concerns. Attachment to sin hampers a person's longing for God and the ability to love. Christian recovery focuses on salvation in and through the grace offered by the unchanging God of love. His unmerited grace re-forms and reshapes the broken vessel of our nature. Salvation in Christ means recovering the image of God that has been defaced by sin. Since we were created in the image of God and God is love, only love fully restores the image. "All our anxieties are ultimately fear of losing love and of the total isolation that follows from this."[1] Recovery, then, is about the freedom to love, which dispels all evil, washes guilt away, restores lost innocence, and brings mourners joy; it casts out hatred, brings us peace, and humbles earthly pride. Sin, on the other hand, impairs the capacity of reason to see and of the heart to love and replaces love with selfish desire.

One might ask, why study the seven deadly sins in the context of twelve-step recovery? The question, however, is crucial. I believe it gives us answers as to why the war on drugs is a failure. Note some statistics: In 2009, there were 77,971 emergency department visits for drug-related suicide attempts among males.[2] It is estimated that state and federal governments in the United States spend more than $15 billion per year, and insurers at least another $5 billion per year, on substance-abuse treatment.[3] It is the opinion of this author that a lack in moral formation is at the root of this crisis. Spiritual growth cannot be limited to psychological issues alone. This book is a response to the question that has emerged from these statistics: what value has moral behavior for recovery? Popular modern psychiatry most often never broaches the subject of sin and dismisses vice as a remnant of the Dark Ages of Christian fundamentalism. Instead, many seek simply the physical and psychological aspects of addiction, but never the moral. Those who do not believe in Christian moral values are bound to be imperfect guides and will fail in some of the most urgent problems related to the human condition concerning moral evil.[4] The secular culture isn't interested in moral questions as such and carries on meaningless debates about drug usage and addiction, failing to admit the unsustainable and ubiquitous effects of immoral behavior that prevent inner liberation for the freedom to love and be loved. Moral weakness is conducive to addiction and codependency. The addict is unable to choose real love. Christianity offers a willed commitment to a way of life that heals human wounds and rectifies the effects of sin while building character that grows in the measure that the person depends on truth and grace. It is in this context that I offer this book for twelve steppers. Governed both by reason and by revelation, the serious Christian soul trained in virtue is able to withstand the assaults of sin by building moral defenses against ever-present temptations, temptations even more omnipresent because of the Internet.

The steps, derived from 2,000 years of lived Christian experience, are twelve practical principles that, lived one day at a time in union with Christian moral principles, lead a person to freedom, happiness, and mental health. They have little efficacy if they are withdrawn from the context of moral goodness. For this reason, in the discussion of Step Four in AA's book on the twelve steps and twelve traditions, which presents an explicit view of the principles of recovery,[5] the reader is asked to inventory the seven deadly sins in his life. AA regards one's character defects reflected in these sinful tendencies and dealing with them in all honesty as necessary for recovery. It was, after all, a culture of Judeo-Christian[6] morality that gave birth to the twelve-step movement.[7] The movement arose at a time when America was a decidedly Christian culture that regarded moral values as part of the call to lead a good life. The founders of our country were convinced of the need for moral formation in order to exist as a free country.[8] Without a desire for moral goodness, Christians are deprived of the heavenly oil to light their lamps (Matthew 25:1–13), which ensures their freedom. If the kingdom of evil abides in a person, he[9] cannot understand God, nor can he understand the dignity of all men and women. People become objects of his pursuit, whether those pursuits be material, monetary, or sexual. That the United States has become a major exporter of pornography, has more people incarcerated than any other so-called developed nation, has an increasing rate of suicide (climbing steadily since 1999) and has the largest population of serial killers than anywhere else on earth, is lost upon a culture that fails to promote moral values. The media seem uninterested in the reasons for the rise of such monstrous behavior as serial killers, killer moms, or child killers. Nor does the media seemed interested in a real solution. This lack of serious interest in moral goodness in the formation of character cannot but have a negative impact on the twelve-step movement. Instead of a movement for spiritual, physical, and moral wellbeing, it can become a therapy session, purely and simply. There is nothing wrong with good therapy, but in and of itself it is not redemptive. Redemption can be had only by genuine love of and desire for moral goodness.

The twelve-step movement arose from Christian principles among those who recognized the redemptive power of a moral life, without which recovery from addiction would be superficial at best. The search for liberty in an ever-increasing culture of servitude cannot be achieved unless grounded in valid moral principles, precisely because a moral way of life is what ensures freedom.

This study of the seven deadly sins is meant for Christians in various stages of recovery from the effects of sin in their lives, sins that lead to addiction and codependency. It takes as its point of departure Christian moral values as legitimate. It is not the intention of this study to convince people of the need for moral formation; rather, taking moral values as necessary to character formation, it studies the deadly sins so as to present the sincere believer with an understanding of virtue and its extremes so that recovery can be deeply grounded, life-enhancing, and redemptive. Because the seven deadly sins predispose us to love wrongly, only when we are weaned from our distorted desires are we free to love rightly.

Chapter One

Recovery Grounded in Christian Truth

> *O Lord, who may abide in your tent? Who*
> *may dwell on your holy mountain? Whoever*
> *walks without blame, doing what is*
> *right, speaking truth from the heart.*
>
> Psalms 15:1–2[10]

Once I met a man who, in pursuit of a new relationship, abandoned his twelve-step meetings. After the relationship ended, he returned to his meetings but with a discouraged attitude. "The steps really don't work," he lamented. But the real issue was his inability to see a connection between his immoral behavior with a series of girlfriends and his lack of recovery through living the steps. Another man came to the Sacrament of Confession consistently confessing sins of lust. When told about the use of the twelve-steps for sexual sobriety, he abruptly interrupted and proudly noted that he was a longtime member of AA. There are many who never seem to have given serious thought and practice to step twelve, wherein a decision is made to practice these principles *in all our affairs*. As it did for the founders of AA, it means sexual affairs as well as drug and alcohol affairs. I have a friend who has sponsored women who are daughters of women she has sponsored, so long has been her involvement in AA. Based upon this experience, when a young woman asks that she be her sponsor, she says yes provided the directee agrees to several rules of behavior: one being "no relationships for one year"—and this for someone trying to recover from alcoholism. Is there a connection?

Moral Values and Mental Health

Mental health comes from doing what is right—the good thing, the moral thing. To the extent that we default on our humanity, we end up with deep psychological consequences, often exchanging one addiction for another. If the seven deadly sins rule our lives, then we become vulnerable to addictive behavior and end up slaves to those addictions. The devastating impact on marriage and family life is only too evident.[11] The importance of good moral habits is crucial to mental health, stable family situations, and character formation.

Viktor Fankl,[12] writing as a psychiatrist about his experiences in the Nazi concentration camps, notes that it was those prisoners who had lost their hold on moral and spiritual values who were the ones who fell victim to the dehumanizing influences of the camps.[13] What most frightened the prisoners was not their external situation in and of itself, but how they thought about it. The interpretation of a person's situation has a great impact on survival. We cannot choose our circumstances in life but we can choose our responses to them. There is a saying heard in twelve-step meetings that goes, "You don't have to react just because you're provoked." But we often let our emotions get in the way of an appropriate response to abusive situations. When something happens to disturb us, the only thing in our power is our response. We can accept it or resent it. It can be a bitter wound or, with Christ, a sacred wound. This is the difference in the response of a person with deep faith and one who only practices his faith in a superficial way, or has no faith at all.

The less effective our natural capacity for happiness is because of sin, the more driven we are to seek escape through drugs, alcohol, food, and other inordinate attachments. Christianity has always recognized the effects of the fall on human nature and human capabilities and the consequent need of Christ as healer. This knowledge is lost on modern psychology—often ideologically tinted—that seeks an explanation for the plight of wounded man simply in childhood trauma, sexual urges, or emotional discomfort. For these reasons then, a study of the seven deadly sins will help the Christian in recovery to understand how Gospel moral principles aid recovery.

Man's Wounded Nature

It is a doctrine of Christianity that all of us have inherited a wounded nature. Scripture attests to this fact when St. Paul notes, "Therefore, just as through one person sin entered the

3

world, and through sin, death, and thus death came to all, inasmuch as all sinned" (Romans 5:12). The integrity of our human nature is wounded because of Adam's transgression, such that our will is weak in the face of evil, we find great difficulty in acquiring truth since sin darkens the intellect, and we have a strong desire to satisfy our senses. All our feelings and emotions were intended by God to be at the service of well-ordered love. One glance at the evening news makes it only too evident that man readily puts his passions at the service of evil. In the state of fallen nature, man opposes himself to the God of love whose moral laws are often perceived as a deterrent to happiness. His laws are regarded as obstacles to fun and pleasure, as the devil entices us to believe. In truth, however, moral law is given for the sake of genuine love, as penal law is for the common good.

Because of our wounded nature, we are in the need of grace, which restores us to the beauty in which man was created before the fall of Adam. In the sense that we are all wounded and in need of redemption, we are not whole, nor fully normal. Normal man is redeemed man, i.e., man as he was created to be by God. We should note that statistics do not determine what normal behavior is. This is often a trick of propagandists who have vested interest in getting people to believe their propaganda.[14] Because man is fallen, we cannot use the most numerous type as normal. Normal is what human nature was created to be. Because Jesus did not inherit Adam's wounded nature, He is the perfect exemplar of man's natural being and manifests the nature of normal. He becomes the standard by which we measure ourselves.[15]

Regarding man's woundedness, the Vatican II document *Gaudium et Spes* explains:

What Revelation makes known to us is confirmed by our own experience. For when man looks into his own heart he finds that he is drawn towards what is wrong and sunk in many evils which cannot come from his good creator. Often refusing to acknowledge God as his source, man has also upset the relationship which should link him to his last end, and at the same time he has broken the right order that should reign within himself as well as between himself and other men and all creatures.[16]

It is by our Christian faith that we know God created man in His image and established him in His friendship. A spiritual creature, man can live this friendship only in free submission to God by living in faith, hope, and love (cf. *Catechism of the Catholic Church* #396, #1812).[17] Man, however, tempted by the devil, let his trust in his Creator die in his heart and, abusing his freedom, disobeyed the God of love (*CCC* #397). Sin then is disobedience toward God and lack of trust in His love.

In sin, man prefers himself to God and by serious sin scorns God. In Adam "man chose himself over and against God, against the requirements of his creaturely status and therefore against his own good. Constituted in a state of holiness, our first parents were destined to be fully "divinized" by God in glory. Seduced by the devil, they wanted to "be like God," but "without God, before God, and not in accordance with God" (*CCC* #398, quoting St. Maximus the Confessor).

As a consequence of original sin, the whole man, body and soul, has been thrown into confusion, though man's nature itself remains the same, for it is a wound not intrinsic to the human intellect and will. He is simply wounded and in need of healing. Even after original sin, man can know by his intellect the fundamental natural and religious truths, and the moral principles by which he should live. He can also perform good works. That is why we speak rather of a *darkening* of the intellect and of a *weakening* of the will, of "wounded" faculties, and not of a loss of their essential capacities. Thus our capacity to make correct judgments has been wounded, making the discovery of truth more difficult. Nothing makes this more evident than the Nazi belief in the superiority of the Aryan race, with the greatest threat to that race being the Jews. The Nazis were not pretending. They actually believed this. We are so easily swayed by what caters to our fallen nature and the wounds of sin, especially the capital sin of pride. Often we choose the path of least resistance and do not sufficiently search for the truth as we should, especially when we have a vested interest is something, as St. Augustine notes when he says, "Whether he will or no, a man is necessarily a slave to the things by means of which he seeks to be happy. He follows them wherever they lead, and fears anyone who seems to have the power to rob him of them."[18] All this helps to explain why Jesus established a *teaching* Church that we might attain certainty about the truth in all that pertains to our salvation. "Ignorance of the fact that man has a wounded nature inclined to evil gives rise to serious errors in the areas of education, politics, social action, and morals" (*CCC* #407). The wounded nature of man is described by St. Paul as the working of four forces within man: the law of the members, the law of sin and death, the law of the mind, and the law of the spirit of life.

The Seat of the Conflict

Once the harmony of man's nature lost its subjection to the unchanging God of love, disorder resulted. St. Paul explains this disorder in the seventh chapter of Romans. He sees that man is not one with himself.[19] There is an inner conflict in man that is deeper than the conflict between the flesh and the spirit. In the very depths of man's being, man is not one with himself. The executive branch and the legislative branch of man's soul are in open conflict, but yet only in one area. In all other areas, the mind and the will agree. Can you imagine anyone having deeply held political convictions going into the voting booth on election day and voting in opposition to those deeply held convictions, explaining that he just couldn't help himself? If someone shows up for work naked and explains how he attempted to clothe himself but just couldn't do it, we would assume him mad. In cases such as these, the will ordinarily obeys the mind. It is only in the moral sphere—the most important area of man's life, that which concerns good and evil, man's salvation or damnation—that the will refuses to obey. These paradoxes are so common in our moral life that we hardly ever give it deeper thought. We often say, "I'm only human," as if it were human to go contrary to what we know to be right.[20] The mind sees and delights in what is good, and yet the will choses what is evil. "I take delight in the law of

God, in my inner self," says St. Paul, "but I see in my members another principle at war with the law of my mind, taking me captive to the law of sin that dwells in my members" (Romans 7:21–22). The drug addict or alcoholic, knowing he is ruining his life, his marriage, his profession, still does it! How can we account for such madness? St. Paul traces this to four laws at work in man. These forces work in pairs: two work for man's good and two for his ruination.

The Law of the Members and the Law of Sin and Death

According to St. Paul there is a law working in us resulting in behavior not in itself sinful but which prepares for sin. This Paul calls the law of the members. In her novel *The Master of Hestviken,* Sigrid Unset, awarded the Nobel Prize for literature in 1928, tells of the bishop's warning to the main character, Olav: if a person decides he will do whatever he wants to do, he will end up seeing the day when he will have done what he never wanted to do.

Some years ago I was invited by a fellow Dominican to give a parish mission in Vienna, Virginia. I wasn't keen on going, since it meant traveling across the country from the West Coast to the East Coast, but after acquiring another mission in the area, I went. One day, an elderly woman asked if Father and I would like to come to her house for dinner. We accepted the offer, and, before dinner, while visiting with her and her guests, I asked how many children she had. She said she had six boys. Poor thing, I thought; no girls! "No girls?" I asked.

Her face fell; she lowered her head and said, "I did have one daughter, but she was murdered. She was murdered by my son who is now in prison."

I could hardly believe it. "I know your son, Marcus Reagan," I said.

"How do you know my son?"

I explained that I had a twelve-step Web site and that I had heard from her son, etc. As a teenager, someone had encouraged Marcus to imbibe some alcoholic drink, which he became very attached to, for he was quite shy and it helped him cope. To shorten the story,[21] Marcus became an alcoholic and drug addict. After many attempts to get him help, his parents gave up. However, his only sister decided to do whatever she could to help Marcus, and so she took him into her home. One evening, high on drugs, he stabbed her to death. Her last words to him were, "Marcus, God forgives you." About a year after Marcus' sentencing, his father died of cancer. Found among his things was a holy card given him by his daughter. Prophetically written on the back was, "Dad, I have offered my life for Marcus' salvation," dated the very day she died! Little did she think that that very day she would actually die to set her brother free, yet free he became.

If a person decides he will do whatever he wants to do—without submitting himself to any acts of self-denial—he will end up seeing the day when he will have done what he never wanted to do. Isn't this the case with scandalous clergy? Imagine the day of their ordination and the pride of their parents, neither thinking of scandal or jail. How does it happen? There is a force in man that leads to sin, a tendency not directly sinful but preparing man for sin, which St. Thomas refers to as the first movements of sin. If this force is allowed to have full sway, it will bring the person under the dominion of the law of sin. St. Paul calls this the law of the members, often referred to as "concupiscence." It is that force in man that says, "Have another drink"; "Sleep a little longer"; "Take the easy way out." Some acts of self-indulgence that are not sinful in and of themselves but which, if indulged in time and again without any self-denial, will end up making the person a slave to the law of sin and death. Take the deadly sin of gluttony from which so many Americans suffer. An obese/alcoholic/ drug-addicted person is ruining his life and knows it but won't stop. He has become a slave to the law of sin and death. Sin can only gain a footing when the law of the members is allowed to have full play.

What is needed to confront this force is a disciplined life, as exemplified in the twelve steps of AA. Only a spiritual program such as this will enable a person to resist the assaults of addiction. A person who gives himself over to the law of the members will eventually find himself a slave to the law of sin and death. Jesus drew the picture of the prodigal son knowing it to be a common human tragedy. Little does the prodigal son imagine he will end up losing everything and eating with pigs. Hitting bottom, however, the prodigal son finds a way out.

The Law of the Mind and the Law of the Spirit of Life

There are two forces working together for the good of man's soul, what St. Paul calls the law of the mind and the law of the spirit. Everyone has an inner voice that always speaks for his good and seeks to lift him up to all that is good and true. This is the voice of conscience. "You shouldn't be looking at this," it says to the pornography user; "You shouldn't have another drink," it says to the problem drinker. Can we say, however, that the person simply has to listen to the voice of conscience and he will be delivered? No. The commands of conscience are beyond his ability to obey. He is a slave. To say to a slave that all he has to do to get free is "just say no" is to lead him into despair. He can't say no. If you envision a heavy stream of water making its way through a channel and you suddenly put up a blockade, will it suffice? The pressure of the water will eventually build up, exerting too much power, and break through. What is needed is the digging of another channel. This is what twelve-step recovery offers: a spiritual program of twelve-step recovery together with an experienced guide—a sponsor—who has lived the steps. This leads the soul to its deliverer, the law of the spirit of life, as St. Paul expresses it (Romans 8:2). God alone can deliver the person from slavery to the law of sin and death, attested to by AA's third step, wherein the person makes a decision to turn his will and life over to the care of God.

Man stands in need of redemptive grace. The grace of a practical spiritual program is needed in order to bring the will into conformity with the truth. The founders of AA recognized the spiritual dimension of recovery. The twelve-step movement offers the ascetical principles for such a spiritual program. No one grows spiritually through the practice of the principles outlined in the twelve steps except by acquiring true spiritual insight into fundamental moral principles. Man yearns for love, but in the yearning gets lost in false substitutes. Recovering man needs clear moral principles to safeguard and ground his sobriety. The struggle to overcome these deep divisions of the soul and to bring our lives into harmony with the Gospel is called asceticism, from a Greek work meaning "combat." It involves spiritual warfare. The founders of AA recognized the disease of alcoholism as a spiritual problem, calling for a spiritual solution. The twelve steps involve a daily regimen of ascetical practices that guide the troubled person to recovery. The Christian knows recovery to be not an end in itself but a means to purify the human heart for love's sake.

The Way Out: Christian Asceticism and the Steps

The struggle against the deadly sins is part of the asceticism of our Christian life. These deadly sins are often themes in great literature because they are the common lot of wounded man and each of us is involved in the struggle to overcome their malice. Twelve-step recovery assumes we are integrating the principles of each step *in all our affairs*—not simply those of a particular addiction, such as drinking or drugs or food. A study of the seven deadly sins will help us understand our ineffectual behavior and lessen our risk of acting out in addictive behavior, or in switching one addiction for another in a revolving circle that goes nowhere.

The seven deadly sins—pride, envy, anger, sloth, avarice, gluttony, and lust—are really inclinations or vices that underlie sins, whether mortal or venial. They derive from Sacred Scripture[22] and were explicated by early monks such as Evagrius of Pontus (345–399) and John Cassian (360–435), and later systematized by Pope St. Gregory the Great (540–504).[23] They provide keys to understanding our character defects. If we understand how they factor into who we have become, we would understand much more about ourselves and the sources of our ineffective behavior. They are often called "capital sins" because they engender other sins. Although not found as a list in Sacred Scripture, they are found all through it, from Genesis to Revelation. The New Testament mentions all of them.

This study is intended to aid the Christian (indeed any person of good will) in understanding the nature of the seven deadly sins and how they inhibit recovery. We investigate the true nature of each sin that it might be more clearly recognized and, hopefully, avoided and healed through the grace of a practical spiritual program. And in considering each deadly sin, we also take into consideration its antidote, that virtue that restrains it. Since virtue is the mean between extremes, we will also look at each deadly sin's opposite extreme. Without nourishing a life of virtue, a person is never free to love, and love is the foundation of immortality.

Chapter Two

The Nature of Love and Sin

> *Love is patient, love is kind. It does not envy,*
> *it does not boast, it is not proud. It is not rude,*
> *it is not self-seeking, it is not easily angered,*
> *it keeps no record of wrongs. Love does not*
> *delight in evil but rejoices with the truth. It*
> *always protects, always trusts, always hopes,*
> *always perseveres. Love never fails.*
>
> I Corinthians 13:4–8

Man was created for life and happiness. All his human urges manifest this. This is as true of the atheist as it is of the man of faith. No sane person wants to die. To discover that one has inoperable cancer and only a few months to live is a dark trauma, both for the atheist and the believer. We want life. We want happiness. And not in mere crumbs but abundantly. Yet life here doesn't satiate all our cravings. All we get are crumbs. We always crave still more. Take the example of music. A person has a great passion for music. He has his favorite types of music and favorite artists. Hearing a new song on the car radio, he longs to hear it again, so much so that he purchases the CD so that he can listen to that song all he wants. Soon, however, he tires of it and puts it aside with the hundreds of CDs he already owns. But a new CD by his favorite singer has come out. Oh, he's got to have it! And so he buys that CD. How many new songs are enough? He will be acquiring new songs until he dies. It's never enough. This is the basis of addiction—a prevailing craving for more. We were created by and directed toward the Infinite. God alone can satisfy human longing because God alone is infinite. Ultimately nothing finite can satisfy—thus Saint Augustine's famous remark, "You have made us for Yourself, O Lord, and our hearts are restless until they find their rest in You."[24] The atheist, who recognizes these desires in himself, has no explanation except to say that nature is cruel, whereas Christianity "solves the unbearable contradiction that runs right through the very form of man"[25] while at the same time civilizing man.

Ultimately addiction is idolatry—the attempt to find fulfillment in finite things. When we attempt to satiate our inborn desire for God by false substitutes that ultimately cannot fulfill, we suffer codependency and addiction. The way out is a life of virtue, and virtue in its most concise definition is rightly ordered love,[26] which alone leads to happiness and life—eternal happiness and eternal life. Divine revelation reveals that love is man's origin and love is his fulfillment in heaven, for he was created by God and God is love (1 John 4:8)—the love by which we love. Thus is love the greatest of the virtues. The reason for the gift of faith is love; with the virtue of hope we take the risk of loving all people as God already does. Pope Benedict notes: "Love is the foundation of immortality, and immortality proceeds from love alone."[27] If I want to be immortally happy, I must learn to love as God loves. Love is the essential principle of the spiritual life. As St. Paul preaches, without love everything else is useless (cf. 1 Corinthians 13:1–13). It is the hallmark of the Christian soul. Jesus teaches, "By this all men will know that you are My disciples, if you have love for one another" (John 13:35). Mother Teresa liked to say, "Love is a fruit in season at all times and within the reach of every hand."[28] But how is love to be understood by the Christian?

The Christian Understanding of Love

When we speak of love, we are speaking in a Christian sense. It is not understood in the same way for all cultures. For the culture of Hollywood, for example, love is purely and simply a feeling, an emotion. Thus people easily fall in and out of false love. They separate and divorce because they no longer feel the same about each other. But soon they have those same feelings or attractions again, but for someone else. This time it is the real connection, they feel. And they hitch up, but lo and behold the feelings fade and the couple separates. Hugh Hefner (founder of *Playboy Magazine*) is a prime example. Crystal Harris, the woman with whom he was most recently involved and to whom he was engaged (she broke off the engagement five days before the wedding day) could have been Hugh's granddaughter! He was sixty when she was born. His first marriage took place in 1949, and here we are well into the third millennium and he's still at it. If God's love for us was an imitation of this sort of love, based on ephemeral feelings, He long ago would have abandoned mankind. Is it any wonder that children growing up in a culture that condones the serial marriages of their parents acquire a conception of love that is so superficial, based purely on feelings? Is it any wonder that the culture of Hollywood breeds addiction and suicide?

For the Christian, love is a virtue and it exists, not in feelings as such, but in the will. I can't make myself feel good about people, especially troublesome people or enemies, but I can still love them, which is to say I bear them no ill *will*. I want what is best for them, despite how I feel about them. Parents may feel angry and upset about their children's behavior, but that doesn't mean they've stopped loving them because their feelings at the moment are rather negative. Feelings prove nothing about love. True love in marriage—at least for the Christian—is meant to mirror Christ's love for His bride, the Church: in sickness and in health, in good times and in bad, until death. We are created for this enduring love and cannot attain happiness without it. An understanding of how feelings and emotions figure into our moral life is important. Dr. Alice Von Hildebrand notes, "Many do not know how to gauge their emotions; they cannot distinguish between valid and invalid feelings. They do not know for certain whether they are truly in love or whether they are animated by wishful thinking and believe themselves in love because they crave the excitement that love gives. They confuse 'loving' with having a crush"[29] and easily fall in and out of "love."

The Role of the Passions

The inability to own one's feelings and deal with them in an appropriate way is often at the root of addiction. The addict uses his drug to anesthetize his feelings and emotions (traditionally referred to as passions). He may, for example, deny to himself his feelings of loneliness. In recovery and without his drug, he becomes acutely aware of the devastating feeling of loneliness. But with encouraging friends in recovery he learns a healthy way to deal with those feelings. Recovery from addiction entails getting in touch with feelings and becoming aware of the role they play in one's life. A twelve-step meeting helps a person emerge from isolation by sharing how he feels. By sharing what he has kept secret for so long, he begins to feel a lot better about himself. There's an expression among twelve steppers that says, "We are only as sick as our secrets." And sick families have secrets. With the support of an anonymous fellowship, a person can own up to how he feels, for there is another saying that goes, if you don't feel your feelings, you act them out.

Often when you ask a person about a decision he's made, the response given is, "I *felt* that..." People make decisions based on how they feel—at the moment! Feelings are important but they are, of themselves, ephemeral. They are part and parcel of the expression of our moral lives, and they are not wrong as such. What can be wrong, however, is allowing them to make our decisions. That which should guide our actions is reason, not emotion without serious reflection. Augustine explains, "If the will is wrongly directed, the emotions will be wrong; if the will is right, the emotions will be not only blameless, but praiseworthy."[30]

All feelings are real, but not all are valid. For example, I feel jealous. The feeling per se is not wrong, but it is wrong for me to compare myself to others, which results in my feeling less than others. Jealousy in most contexts is not reasonable. I can make the decision to stop comparing myself to others and slowly discover my own true worth, which comes from the unchanging God of love. Everything else is vanity. Finding my true worth in God, I do not have to consider myself less than when someone is smarter, taller, more athletic than I.

It is wrong to allow our feelings and emotions to make our decisions apart from reasonable reflection about the truth of the matter. When decisions are made on the basis of how we feel at the moment, we often live to regret it. When our decisions are motivated by right thinking, then they are good and fulfill the aspirations of my passions. "A happy life and a virtuous life are synonymous. Happiness and personal fulfillment are the natural consequences of doing the right thing."[31] Until we realize and act upon this, we will continue to substitute false, fleeting, finite goods based on momentary feelings instead of sound moral truths that lead to pervasive happiness and true freedom.

Sin and the Will

It is not uncommon for people to confess their feelings and emotions as if they were sinful in and of themselves. The *Catechism of the Catholic Church* explains that the passions (i.e. feelings and emotions) have no moral value as such (*CCC* #1767). They are not morally good, nor are they morally bad. What gives them a moral component is what we do about them. All sin lies in the will, i.e., in what a person freely choses to do. Exercising free will is where a person can sanctify his feelings in acting virtuously or pervert them with vice. This is a crucial truth to embrace in order for the Christian to know and understand himself. Once morally good choices are made, our feelings follow and share in virtue.

Since the will is dependent on the intellect to make its decision, it is important to know the truth. Sin darkens the intellect so that there is no clear perception of the truth. It can be said that sin gives a bias against the truth and debilitates reason. We are already born with a wound that keeps us in darkness until we are enlightened by the grace of faith. Thus do we say that Christ is the light that came into the darkness to help us see in truth (John 8:12). He tells us of the man born blind (John 9:1–41) as a reference to the fallen state of all the wounded children of Eve. Sin impairs the capacity of reason to see. "Know the truth," says Christ, " and the truth will set you free" (John 8:32). By knowing the truth about ourselves and our emotions, we can discover ways to mature and gain the emotional equilibrium and healthy balance we need to take charge of our lives, grow closer to Christ, and share in the joy of His love. The relevance of understanding the role of the passions in daily life is evident. Such knowledge is a sure guide to healthy and holy living, for without a proper understanding of the important role played by our passions, a person is truly left in the dark. When people are afraid of owning their emotions, they wear a mask. And if a person denies his feelings, he acts them out. Neglecting to understand how emotional responses are impacted by one's background and temperament, a person is often left feeling hopeless, even despairing, because of unwanted feelings. We do a great service to the Christian community—indeed to any person of good will—by explicating the role of emotions and pointing the way to emotional equilibrium.[32]

Emotions informed by virtue are part of our human existence whereby "man intuits the good and suspects evil" (*CCC* #1771). Because a person's temperament, his inner wounds, and his life experiences profoundly influence his emotional responses, he needs to learn how to mature his emotions so that they do not make his decisions for him contrary to right reason. Through recovery in living the spirituality of the steps, he can be in control of his responses no matter what emotions come into play. The important role given by an anonymous fellowship such as AA is evident. It is a safe haven where people learn by others' sharing their experience, strength, and hope. In the safe environment of those meetings, they find the help and inspiration they need as they learn to express how they feel.[33]

We only have to look at the daily news to see how so many adults are controlled by their emotions and respond in inappropriate ways to threatening situations because they have never learned to mature their emotions. Given our contemporary lack of a lucid study of emotions in light of Christian theology, it is a relief to learn, for example, and as the Church teaches, "strong feelings are not decisive for the morality or the holiness of persons" (*CCC* #1768). Good holy people have a wide expanse of emotions. For example, a saintly and morally chaste person can have deep sexual feelings. The feelings themselves say nothing about the holiness of the person. We are not to suppress our passions but guide them by reason and will. Because the passions are a fundamental part of human life, they need to be directed by grace.

It is surprising that many modern manuals of spiritual direction tend to neglect the role of emotions in human life. This neglect can defeat a person's desire for wholeness. Saint Thomas Aquinas knew this well when he taught, "Being insensitive to our feelings and emotions is a vice."[34] As a result, his study on the moral life includes a section on emotions. The emotional life, which forms a part of our being, has a place in moral reflection, for man does not work out his destiny solely by acts of his free will. Rather, it is with the power of his whole being, body and soul, that he attains his salvation.

As we grow in goodness, we learn to be honest about how we feel and yet not allow our decisions to be made solely on how we feel at the moment. Rather, we act according to the dictates of right reason with input from our feelings. Because our nature is wounded, our feelings and emotions require this guidance of reason. Just as love lies in the will, so does sin. It is quite common for people to come to the Sacrament of Reconciliation and confess their feelings as if they were sins. For example, a woman comes and confesses her feelings of antipathy for her daughter-in-law. She feels so terrible because she cannot stand her daughter-in-law. So she confesses it! Should the confessor say, "For your penance, say three Hail Marys"? Can you picture, then, the woman going out to dinner with her daughter-in-law, the two of them staying up late telling jokes and combing each other's hair?

"I just adore my daughter-in-law!"

"But I thought you couldn't stand her," says a friend.

"Not any more, I went to confession."

Rubbish! The truth is, she still can't stand the woman even after confession! To *feel* antipathy for someone is not sin. To act out of the antipathy and be uncharitable would be the sin. She knows she loves her daughter-in-law because she is good to her, has her best interests at heart, and shows her concern. She bears her no ill will; therefore, there is no sin involved and nothing to confess.

Exercising the virtues perfects both our feelings[35] and the will to do good, and this is what makes for a good person. No one should be praised nor blamed simply for how they feel. Never say to a friend, "You shouldn't feel that way." What are they supposed to do, deny how they feel? The person who feels lonely, afraid, or angry must not be praised nor blamed; rather, we are praised or blamed on account of our virtues or our vices. We need to perfect our feelings with virtue and not act out of them apart from right reason. There is an acronym that says halt: never act if you're hungry, angry, lonely, or tired. We may feel these feelings without choice, but what we do with them is where virtue or vice come into play. The virtues and vices are moral habits and involve choices. Once acquired, these habits dispose a person toward good or toward evil. A psychologically healthy life is not possible for those who have not acquired virtue. Nor is love, correctly understood, possible.

Immorality Kills Love

The love that we call "charity" gives us the awareness of God's love for another person. This awareness of God's presence and other people's legitimate needs is not easily achieved because by our fallen nature we are self-centered. Grace is needed to pierce the hardness of our hearts. The seven deadly sins kill charity's love, or rather, they make genuine love impossible. To achieve our goal, that for which we were created—eternal life and happiness—we need to do battle against sin. Although eternal life is given to us in and through the theological virtues of faith and hope, it is not given us by faith and hope. Divine love alone achieves our eternal happiness. Sin, however, destroys our chances for heaven precisely because it impedes our ability to love.

Sin is a morally bad act—an act not in accord with reason informed by the divine law (cf. *CCC* #1849). "It wounds man's nature and injures human solidarity" (*CCC* #1872). God has endowed us with reason and free will, and He has made us subject to His law, which is known to us by the dictates of our conscience. Our actions must conform with those dictates, otherwise we sin (Romans 14:23). "Sin is an abuse of the freedom that God gives to created persons" (*CCC* #387)— a freedom intended by God for love's sake. Love makes a person Godlike, as Pope Benedict writes: "The vocation of love is what makes the person an authentic image of God: one becomes similar to God to the degree that one becomes one who loves."[36] The Christian is called by Christ to live his moral life in the light of faith, and this faith reveals to him the primacy of love, correctly understood.

The more one does what is good, the freer one becomes. The paradoxical nature of true freedom is highlighted by St. Augustine when he comments on Christ's teaching that to die to oneself is to find oneself. Augustine notes that to part with one's will does not mean we lose freedom; it means we gain freedom in the loss.[37] There is no true freedom except in the service of what is good and just. The choice to disobey and do evil is an abuse of freedom and leads to "the slavery of sin" (Romans 6:17; *CCC* 1733).

Evil itself is a lack of the goodness that ought to be present. If this lack of a good is found in a thing, it is a physical evil; if it is found in the freely willed actions of man, it is moral evil or sin. Evil is merely the defect of goodness and not a positive reality. When the good that ought to be present is missing, there is evil. Thus evil has been defined as the privation of a due good.[38] Sin is nothing else than a morally bad act—an act not in accord with reason but rather one that chases after an apparent good.

Chapter Three

The Seven Capital Sins in General

> For the wages of sin is death, but the gift of
> God is eternal life in Christ Jesus our Lord.
>
> Romans 6:23

Traditionally all sin is related to or flows from the seven
capital sins. "They are called 'capital' because they engender
other sins, other vices" (*CCC* #1866). Their antidotes are the
moral virtues. Each of the virtues under grace directs us to
our ultimate fulfillment: the unchanging God of love. Our
wounded nature, however, acts against our ultimate fulfillment
by seeking satisfaction in substitutes manifest in the vices that
offer pseudo fulfillment. If vice did indeed offer true happiness,
we would be the happiest nation on earth and not one with
such a high rate of incarceration, addiction, and suicide.

The seven deadly sins are sometimes called "capital sins" or
"capital vices." The origin of the word "capital" is from Middle

English for "standing at the head or beginning." Thus they are called "capital sins" because all the sins that we commit are said to flow from them as from a source.[39] When we speak of them as sins, we are speaking of sin in an analogous sense. This means that the so-called deadly sins are not necessarily sinful in themselves; rather, they are sources of sin from which other vices and sins originate. In reality, they are actually vices.[40] The seven deadly sins are opposed to the seven capital virtues.[41]

Like the ancient Greek philosopher Socrates, St. Thomas Aquinas teaches that morality is consistent with the mean between extremes,[42] that a man must know how to choose the mean and avoid the extremes on either side. Below is a chart showing the capital sin, its opposing virtue, and its opposite extreme.

Capital Sin	Opposing Virtue	Opposite Extreme
Pride	Humility	Self-loathing
Envy	Kindness	Pusillanimity
Avarice	Generosity	Wastefulness
Anger	Patience	Servility
Sloth	Diligence	Workaholism
Gluttony	Temperance	Deficiency
Lust	Chastity	Prudishness

In the proceeding chapters we will discuss the deadly sin, its opposing virtue, and its opposite extreme. Here is a short summary of each.

- **Pride** gives birth to an undue and inappropriate appreciation of one's self-worth. It is countered by humility. As pride leads to other sin, true humility clears a path for holiness. It's opposite extreme is self-loathing.

- **Envy,** in contradiction to God's law of love, is manifest in a person's sorrow and distress over the good fortune of another person. It is countered by kindness. Kindness and brotherly love is manifest in the unprejudiced, compassionate, and charitable concern for others. Its opposite extreme is pusillanimity.

- **Avarice** is the sin of inordinate desire for earthly things. It is countered by generosity. The virtue of generosity is focused not merely on the appropriate concern regarding one's earthly things, but furthermore on liberality and a willingness to give, freely and without request for commendation. Its opposite extreme is wastefulness.

- **Anger** is also called wrath or rage. It is countered by patience or meekness. Where the sin of wrath is about quick temper and unnecessary vengeance, the virtue of meekness focuses on patiently seeking appropriate resolution to conflicts, and on the ability to forgive and show mercy. Its opposite extreme is servility or "doormathood."

- **Sloth** as a capital sin refers to an oppressive sorrow that so weighs upon a person that he does not seek the good he ought. It is countered by diligence or persistence. Its opposite is workaholism.

- **Gluttony** is countered by the virtue of temperance or abstinence.[43] To be gluttonous is to overindulge. On the opposite hand, the virtue of temperance is centered on self-control and moderation. Its opposite extreme is deficiency.

- **Lust** is an inordinate desire for sexual pleasure. It is countered by chastity, which embraces moral wholesomeness and purity, and in both thought and action treats God's gift of sexuality with due reverence and respect. Its opposite extreme is prudishness.

The seven deadly sins are vices. Their antidotes are virtues.

Virtue and Vice

Virtue and vice signify habits. All habits are acquired by repeated behavior. The same is true of artistic habits, like playing the piano or learning to knit. At first it is difficult, but with time and practice, it becomes so easy that a person hardly has to concentrate. It is the same with the moral virtues. They become second nature to us. But to become readily virtuous takes time and effort. An individual sin as such is not yet a habit; it is the repeating of the sin that becomes a habit. Virtues or vices are caused or acquired by frequently repeated acts. They become deeply rooted patterns of behavior.

When one acquires a virtue, one has an habitual and firm disposition to do good. It allows the person not only to perform good acts freely and easily, but to make the most of himself. The virtuous person tends toward the good with all his sensory and spiritual powers; he pursues the good and chooses it in concrete actions (*CCC* #1803). One of the properties of virtue is that it lies as a mean between the extremes of excess and deficiency. One vice goes too far; the other vice comes up short. Virtue is the golden mean between the extremes and is in conformity with reason.

The moral life isn't simply a matter of the capital vices versus the life of virtue. Rather, virtue stands between extremes. We must keep this in mind when discussing the deadly sins and their opposite virtues, that there exists an extreme on each side of the virtue. For example, chastity is a virtue that stands between the extremes of lust and prudishness or insensitivity.[44] Lacking this knowledge leads some to conclude that to be chaste is to be as cold as ice, whereas in reality coldness is the other extreme. A prude who becomes slighted at any breach of decorum is not virtuous. In reality, chastity and tender affection are not mutually exclusive. It is often the case for persons to go from one extreme to the other and think themselves virtuous—from lust addict to prude, from drug fanatic to religious fanatic.

We can see this point in a remark made by Fr. Dubay about Chinese convert John Wu. As Fr. Dubay points out, Mr. Wu was struck that highly desirable traits were not mutually exclusive. He saw this in the life of St. Thérèse. "Wu concluded," Fr. Dubay reports, "that the Church that could produce a Thérèse has to be the home of the divine on earth, for he found in this young woman 'a living synthesis of such opposite extremes as humility and boldness, freedom and discipline, joy and suffering, duty and love, strength and tenderness, grace and nature, wisdom and folly, wealth and poverty, community and individuality.'"[45]

St. Augustine situates the life of virtue in the context of love, for without virtue, love is not possible, and without love salvation is not possible. Regarding the four cardinal virtues of temperance, courage, justice, and prudence, Augustine teaches:

"I hold that virtue is nothing other than the perfect love of God. Now, when it is said that virtue has a fourfold division, as I understand it, this is set according to the various movements of love…We may, therefore, define these virtues as follows: temperance is love preserving itself entire and incorrupt for God; courage is love readily bearing all things for the sake of God; justice is love serving only God, and therefore ruling well everything that is subject to the human person; prudence is love discerning well between what helps it toward God and what hinders it."[46]

In this study we will look not only at the capital vices but the virtue that frees us from sin and death. We start with the first of the deadly sins—pride—which is found to a greater or lesser degree in all sin, as seen in the expression, "Pride comes before a fall" (Proverbs 16:18). Thus will we spend more time with this sin and its remedy than the other six.

Chapter Four

Pride, Humility, and Self-loathing

> *When pride comes, disgrace comes, but*
> *with the humble is wisdom.*
>
> Proverbs 11:2

Mr. Darcy and Elizabeth Bennet in *Pride and Prejudice* are prime examples of the capital vice of pride at work in their lives, a pride that gives birth to prejudice. Mr. Darcy struggles against his romantic feelings for Elizabeth Bennet because of her inferior social status. His pride precludes any relationship with her, and he even works against his good friend, Bingley, from developing a relationship with Elizabeth's sister, Jane, for the same reason. When the truth is made known of Mr. Darcy's involvement in saving the Bennett family from disgrace over the situation of Lydia with Mr. Wickham, Elizabeth is able to see past her pride and prejudice regarding Mr. Darcy. Likewise with Mr. Darcy. With the gaining of humility through honesty and truth, love is able to triumph over pride and prejudice. Love is by nature humble because love transcends an excess of self-preoccupation.

In early Christian monasticism, pride and vainglory overlapped and were often listed together, whereas for St. Thomas, they are kept distinct. For our purposes we will treat them as one. In general, however, with vainglory a person attempts to show off as he seeks recognition and adulation from others for his own glory while with pride he takes credit for his accomplishments apart from God. The remedy for both is humility.

Humility stands between the extremes of pride and self-loathing. One might think that humility is opposed to magnanimity, but St. Thomas explains that, "Humility restrains the will from aiming at great things against right reason, while magnanimity urges the mind to great things in accord with right reason. Hence it is clear that magnanimity is not opposed to humility: indeed they concur in this, that each is according to right reason."[47] The distortion of pride comes when we either attribute to ourselves what is, in reality, a gift or exaggerate our gifts. We all have the tendency to acclaim our good actions as our own and blame our bad actions on others or on circumstances. I noticed this as a teacher when returning exams to students with their grades. Those with a good grade automatically exclaimed, "I got an A!" while those with a bad grade equally automatically exclaimed, "He gave me an F!" The credit for the good grade was the person himself, while the reception of the bad grade was the teacher's fault. This is true of the addict who expects praise for his sobriety but not contempt for his drinking. How proud we fallen creatures are! In truth the good that we do is the result of God's grace and mercy, while the evil we do is the manifestation of our true selves without grace.

Bishop Sheen once remarked, "God does not love us because we are lovely or lovable. His love exists not on account of our character but on account of His. Our highest experience is responsive not initiative. And it is only because we are loved by Him, that we are lovable." Similarly did C.S. Lewis write, "The Christian does not think God will love us because we are good, but that God will make us good because He loves us." Pride, on the other hand, wants to be the source of its own excellence. Humility is a peculiarly Christian virtue that keeps man from confusing himself with God. Because of the prevalence of pride in fallen man, the first weapons needed in spiritual warfare are self-distrust and humility.

If a person never experiences the free gift of love (which is what God offers us and we experience either directly or in and through others), the person cannot truly love others. The love a person has for himself is prior to the love he has for anyone else, as Jesus' commandment implies, "Love your neighbor as yourself" (Mark 12:31). Pope John Paul II made this evident when he said, "Man cannot live without love. He remains a being that is incomprehensible for himself...if love is not revealed to him, if he does not encounter love, if he does not experience it and make it his own, if he does not participate intimately in it."[48] Self-love is the origin of the love of neighbor, and the love that a person has for himself is the natural form and root of many loves, including parental love.[49] Without this experience of genuine parental love, the human person is subject to the forces of that original wound of sin in which he was conceived.

Because of that wound, the proud person acts as if he were the source of his own excellence, which is pride. This desire to be the source of one's own excellence was Lucifer's sin. The sin is not in wanting to be like God—for the Lord teaches us to be "perfect as your heavenly Father is perfect" (Matt 5:48)—but rather to be Godlike in and through one's own merits. God alone is the source of His own excellence. The devil has power over us because of our fear of being unlovable. He can provoke this fear in us to keep us from experiencing love. It was the envy of the devil that brought about man's downfall. "Through the envy of the devil, death entered the world" Sacred Scripture warns us (Wisdom 2:24). Knowing that man is offered a place in heaven enrages the devil. The devil hates goodness and hates beauty and seeks with all his power to destroy both. It is difficult to believe that anyone could hate beauty and goodness. Yet you just have to imagine a beautiful and young innocent girl in the presence of evil men. Would these evil men want to protect the beauty of her innocence? Certainly not; each would want to be the first to destroy it. This is great evil. Sin, with its fear of death, has led to our captivity under the devil's power.[50]

The devil's power over us is strengthened because of pride's demand that love must be merited. We are deeply fearful of being unlovable and of dying. These fears can be provoked by the devil who has some power over our memory and imagination (but not our intellect or will). The devil knows authentic love to be the means of destroying his power over us (cf. Luke 10:19; Romans 8:31; Galatians 2:20), and so he provokes fear in us, which keeps us slaves to sin and death. As slaves to deadly sin we are not capable of love, correctly understood.

Christ offers us the path to freedom, which is expressly manifest in the Easter mystery we celebrate each time we attend Holy Mass. The Mass is the complete mystery of salvation, the mystery of Christ's passion, death, and resurrection, which, if embraced by us, frees us from satan's power of sin and death. Saint Peter expresses this theme in his first letter:

Beloved, clothe yourselves with humility in your dealings with on another, for "God opposes the proud but bestows grace on the humble." So humble yourselves under the mighty hand of God, that he may exalt you in due time. Cast all your worries upon him because he cares for you. Be sober and vigilant. Your opponent the Devil is prowling around like a roaring lion seeking for someone to devour" (1 Peter 5: 5—8).

Our Holy Father, Pope Benedict, in speaking of the teachings of Saint Paul on the humility of Christ, makes the following remarks on Paul's famous hymn in the Letter to the Philippians (cf. 2: 6–11). The Pope says:

The structure of this text [of Philippians] illustrates the principal moments of the journey undertaken by Christ. His pre-existence is expressed with the words: "Though he was in the form of God, [he] did not regard equality with God something to be grasped" (verse 6). Afterward follows the voluntary abasement of the Son in second stanza: "He

emptied himself, taking the form of a slave" (verse 7); "He humbled himself, becoming obedient to death, even death on a cross" (verse 8). The third stanza of the hymn announces the response of the Father to the humiliation of the Son: "Because of this, God greatly exalted him and bestowed on him the name that is above every name" (verse 9).

What is impressive is the contrast between the radical abasement and the resulting glorification in the glory of God. It is evident that this second stanza contrasts with the pretension of Adam, who wanted to make himself God, and it contrasts as well with the actions of the builders of the Tower of Babel, who wanted to construct for themselves a bridge to heaven and make themselves divine. But this initiative of pride ended with self-destruction: In this way, one doesn't arrive to heaven, to true happiness, to God. The gesture of the Son of God is exactly the contrary: not pride, but humility, which is the fulfillment of love, and love is divine. The initiative of abasement, of the radical humility of Christ, which contrasts with human pride, is really the expression of divine love; from it follows this elevation to heaven to which God attracts us with his love.[51]

The Pope shows that the evident humiliation that Christ undergoes out of love for sinners models the path of love for us. In a similar way, St. John of the Cross explains: "To be taken with love for a soul, God does not look upon its greatness, but upon the greatness of its humility."[52] The early desert monks and nuns went to the desert not to escape human society but rather to find their true worth. They began their search by facing their own sinfulness. They set out to examine their lives in utter honesty and with deep humility. These desert religious knew that if they wanted to grow in goodness and overcome their defects of character, they would have to grow in humility. Experience taught them that being ready to have God remove a person's defects was in direct proportion to the degree of that person's humility. Abba Alonius, one of the desert fathers, used to say, "Humility is the land where God wants us to go to offer Him sacrifice."[53] The journey to that land, however, is a most difficult one for several reasons.

First, as a result of original sin, we are afraid of humility. We are afraid of humility because we are afraid of being unlovable and afraid of dying. Instead of taking an honest look at myself because of pride's fear, I justify my bad actions or exalt myself in the eyes of others, reinforcing my dependence on the world for my happiness and security. As a result, I can never live an honest straightforward life.

Second, humility is often seen as weakness. One elderly man once told me, "Father, I'm tired of being Christian— people just walk all over you." This poor man had suffered from "wimp-hood" his whole life and never recognized it. He confused weakness and abasement with humility. He confused the other extreme with the virtue itself. This is a common misunderstanding of the virtue of humility. Humility is *not* weakness; it is strength. Arrogant, self-centered people are weak in that they are easily controlled by the opinions and actions of others, but because a humble person is at home with himself and need not impress others, he remains less vulnerable to others' attitudes. Only a humble person can maintain an understanding attitude. And humility is *not* to have a high tolerance for inappropriate behavior. People who tolerate socially unacceptable behavior are weak, not humble. On the other hand, the humble desert monk could love his troublesome neighbor as himself, endure insults as glory, and look upon misery as riches.

One child in a CCD class was asked the definition of humility. "Humility," he answered, "is pretending you're worse than everyone else." Humility is *not* pretense. Many years ago, two of our friars were taking a census for one of our parishes. Suddenly, on the way home, they almost drove off a cliff! What distracted the friar who was driving? The last family they had visited for the census turned out to be great devotees of the Dominican Order and were delighted to meet these two young friars. Now, the friar who was driving was a good artist, and so his companion suggested, "Brother, these people love Dominicans and they love beautiful art. Wouldn't they love to have one of your art pieces?"

"My stuff is junk compared to theirs," he humbly retorted.

"I know it is, but just the same…"

The car screeched across the road as the outraged driver reacted to the negative remark about his artistic abilities. Of course, the critical remark had its intended effect—to reveal his false humility. "A man is never so proud," says C.S. Lewis, "as when striking an attitude of humility."[54] Humility is the truth about myself, no better, no worse than I am. Otherwise it is false humility.

Scripture says, "Conduct your affairs with humility, and you will be loved more than a giver of gifts" (Sirach 3:17). We are taught by this reading that humility invites love. Nothing draws us closer to each other than humility with honesty. The Gospel teaches us that in humility is found exaltation: "Everyone who exalts himself will be humbled, but the one who humbles himself will be exalted" (Luke 14:11). Humility is the antidote of pride. Therefore the baptized person should train himself to be humble, for in humility is great freedom.

The Nature of Humility

Humility is a virtue, and a virtue is a habit. As noted above, one acquires a habit by practice. The more you practice, the easier it becomes. Humility is the foundational virtue of the spiritual life. St. Thomas Aquinas notes, "By way of removing obstacles, humility holds the first place, inasmuch as it casts out pride…In this sense humility is said to be the foundation of the spiritual edifice."[55] There have been many beautiful looking edifices that have come crashing down, scandalizing many people in the process. The foundation was arrogance, not humility, self and not God.

Because humility casts out pride, it is not vulnerable to pride's fear. It doesn't fear someone being thought better of, for humility does not compare. It doesn't fear being unlovable because it knows itself to be undeservedly loved. In the same vein, St. Teresa of Avila teaches that humility is the primary virtue that must be practiced by those who pray. One would think that love is the primary virtue to be practiced, but in all truth, arrogant, self-centered people are incapable of the selflessness that is love, and so humility comes first and removes many obstacles to prayer because prayer concerns a loving relationship with Another. With that said, however, one has to watch for the opposite extreme: self-loathing. St. Teresa cautions against a certain misunderstanding of humility that may cause a person to view himself as worthless:

Beware…against certain types of humility which the devil inculcates in us and which makes us very uneasy about the gravity of our past sins. There are many ways in which he is accustomed to depress us so that in time we withdraw from Communion and give up our private prayer, because the devil suggests to us that we are not worthy to engage in it…The thing gets to such a pass that a soul can be made to believe that, through being what it is, it has been forsaken by God, and thus it almost doubts His mercy…Humility, however deep it may be, neither disquiets nor troubles nor disturbs the soul; it is accompanied by peace, joy, and tranquility… Far from disturbing or depressing the soul, it enlarges it and makes it fit to serve God better.[56]

Humility is a moral virtue that restrains the inordinate desire for one's own excellence. The Gospel gives the example of people who love places of honor at banquets and in church (Matthew 23:6), as if a certain place at table gives a person his basic worth. It's all a matter of vanity and is deeply saddening, for a person's worth doesn't come from the world and what it thinks. Humility is simply the growing awareness that "of my self, I am nothing. The good I do is from God's grace; the evil I do, that is mine." Real humility comes when we stop comparing ourselves to others—as the saying goes: compare, despair. There is always someone smarter, nicer looking, stronger, richer, etc. Humility is an honest assessment of oneself—no better, no worse than I am. With humility we learn to let go of the need to compare ourselves to others. A humble person lives in peace with who he is.

Rare is the person who attributes his success to God. Some take pride in saying, "I had to pull myself up by my own boot straps." Well, who gave you the boots, or the strength to pull yourself up? The illusion that we can live independently of God's grace is healed by genuine humility. Scripture speaks against the pernicious opinion we have of ourselves, whereby we attribute our successes to our own efforts apart from God's grace (cf. Deuteronomy 9:4–5). While a humble person can strive for and achieve great things, he attributes his success to God. The difference between the humble man and the proud man isn't found in the greatness of the deeds they perform, but how they view their success. The proud man wants to be the source of his own excellence while the humble man recognizes his dependence on God for his talents and good deeds. St. Paul makes this clear by asking, "What do you possess that you have not received? But if you have received it, why are you boasting as if you did not receive it?" (I Corinthians 4:7).

St. John Chrysostom notes that God judges a person's conversion not by his efforts but by his humility. He uses the following illustration:

Imagine two chariots. Harness virtue and pride to one, sin and humility to the other. You will see that the chariot drawn by sin outstrips that of virtue…To understand why one of these vehicles is faster than the other, remember the Pharisee and the publican…One relied on this own

43

righteousness, on his own fasting and the tithes he paid. The other needed to say only a few words to be free of all his sins. That was because God was not only listening to his words, He also saw the soul of him who spoke them, and finding it humble and contrite, He judged him worthy of His compassion and love...[57]

There was a story among the desert monks (said to be from a hermitess named Amma Theodora) about a hermit who was able to cast out evil spirits. The hermit had asked the demons, "What makes you go away? Is it fasting?"

They replied, "We do not eat or drink."

"Is it vigils?"

They replied, "We do not sleep."

"Is it separation from the world?"

"We live in the deserts."

"What power sends you away then?"

They said, "Nothing can overcome us, but only humility."

"Do you see how humility is victorious over the demons?"[58]

According to Aquinas, the virtue of humility is part of the cardinal virtue of temperance because it restrains and moderates the "impetuosity of the emotions."[59] When people fail to mature their emotions, integrate them into the life of virtue, and grow in humility, they are often driven by shame. Because a humble person has a good relationship with himself, he is able to reach out to love his neighbor (as he is commanded to do by the Lord, cf. Mark 12:31). A shame-based person is incapable of this.

Self-loathing and Humility

The opposite extreme of pride is self-loathing, sometimes mistaken for genuine humility. Someone might say, "Such a humble person," when in reality that person is not humble at all but is acting out of fear and does good in order to protect himself from criticism and rejection. Today we would say that such a person has a poor self-image or has an inferiority complex. Humility has nothing to do with slavish fear. Such a person is often filled with shame and self-loathing and as a result can never live an honest, straightforward life. St. Thomas makes an effort to teach that genuine self-love, as opposed to selfishness, is a virtue and a grave obligation.[60] If selfishness is due to a lack of genuine self-love, this too comes from pride. A person who does not love himself truly cannot truly love others.

Love is man's fulfillment. When a person does not love himself, he treats his neighbor as himself, which is to say that he will not be able to have a healthy concern for his neighbor's good. St. Catherine remarked that we love others with the same love we see ourselves loved with. If I can accept that I am loved as I am, then I can love you as you are. A genuine love for others is predicated upon a genuine love of self. I cannot avail myself of God's love for me unless I am willing to offer it back to Him as He would have me, but I cannot do that so long as I am victimized by pride. When a person's pride is hurt it begets resentment and self-pity. The founders of Alcoholics Anonymous knew well from experience that unless these two emotions were healed, they would set the alcoholic up to take his drink. Thus, steps six and seven focus on humility as the remedy.

Personality expresses itself in altruism, in reaching out to others and having others relate back. The biblical dictum, "It is not good for man to be alone," (Genesis 2:18) is based on this fact.[61] We are created in the image of God and God is not solitude enclosed upon itself but a Trinity of Persons. To be a person is to exist in relationship to other persons. Created in the image of God, man is by nature a creature whose growth can best be nourished in communion with others. Withdrawal from others does nothing to enrich our human nature as persons. It simply gives momentary relief from the pain of shame but ultimately demeans us a persons. Because a sense of belonging is crucial to mental stability, isolation can create a mental health crisis. Social withdrawal is emotionally and psychologically very costly. There are studies that show that loneliness creates a mental health crisis.[62] If we remain isolated long enough, we lose our sense of self, for it is only in communion with other people that we grow. "Loner" is often part of the profile of serial killers. An FBI study of the serial rapist notes that, "Because of his feelings of inadequacy, any social relationships would be with much younger or less sophisticated women. In general, though…he'd be a loner."[63]

When a person has no adequate self-acceptance, he tends to get involved in unhealthy relationships and ends up blaming the other person when the relationship goes sour. For example, it is not uncommon for healthcare professionals to marry into alcoholic families. Why would this be the case? Because often the person involved in healthcare does so out of the satisfaction that comes from being needed. Some such people confuse being needed with being loved and get involved with people who need them. It is so common for nurses to marry alcoholics that nurses have written a book for nurses titled *I'm Dying to Take Care of You.*[64] Because growing in love grows out of self-acceptance, until one properly loves himself, he cannot love another. Codependent relationships are often based in shame and a lack of true self-esteem.

The Compass of Shame

Dr. Donald Nathanson developed a theory about shame and the human response to it that he calls "The Compass of Shame."[65] When confronted in a negative way with something we've done wrong, and which makes us feel awful about ourselves, we experience a painful feeling of humiliation that we call shame. Rather than taking an honest look at ourselves and digesting the shame in a healthy way, we often resort to one of four varying escape routes.

Withdrawal:
- isolating oneself
- running and hiding

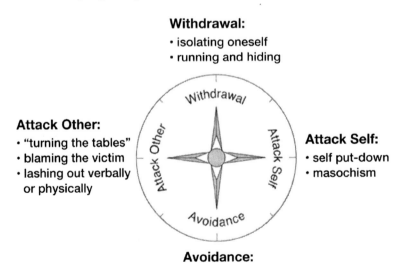

Attack Other:
- "turning the tables"
- blaming the victim
- lashing out verbally or physically

Attack Self:
- self put-down
- masochism

Avoidance:
- denial
- abusing drugs and alcohol
- distraction through thrill-seeking

These patterns of behavior are learned in early childhood and offer us an escape from the negative feeling of shame. Although in the long run, escape inhibits our spiritual well-being and emotional maturity, it feels better than having to take an honest look at ourselves. But as Jesus warns, "Whoever finds his life will lose it, and whoever loses his life for my sake will find it" (Matthew 10:39) in the long run.

At the north end of the compass is "withdrawal." A person disconnects so as not to have to face the shame. Ultimately, of course, it defeats our human need to belong. Withdrawal does nothing to enrich our human nature as persons. It simply gives momentary relief from the pain of shame but ultimately demeans us as persons.

Some of us, however, want to stay connected and fear isolation, and so we incline, emotionally speaking, to the east end of the compass. This way of dealing with the shame is to become falsely submissive by "attacking self." Such a person diminishes himself in the eyes of others and thus manages to evade the shame while taking pleasure in self-pity. In the attempt to avoid the shame, the person becomes adept in the ways of subservience. As one woman who married an abusive man explained, "The rocks in his head fit the holes in mine."

At the south end is the opposite of "Withdrawal"— "Avoidance." The attempt here is to avoid shame by hiding it from consciousness. Addictive behavior helps to hide the shame. Dr. Nathanson believes that shame is avoided by alcohol and covered over by drugs. "These drugs," he says, "which we sometimes call courage in a bottle, prevent the feeling of shame from taking hold. A good stiff drink will ward off the horrible feeling of shame."[66] Living in a culture of severe addiction, Americans seek an unhealthy escape to avoid their demons.

At the west end of the compass is "Attack Others." In recent years there has been an increase in the discussion of bullying, evermore present, especially at schools. The bully expresses his inner shame by attacking others. Demeaning them or putting them down gives temporary relief from his own shame. Hurt people hurt people. Happy people are not likely to harm others. The bully likes to shame others, put them down, and laugh at a their adversities. Unless the bully comes to terms with his own shame, he will always remain a threat to those with whom he lives and works. Such a person will resort to ridiculing others rather than face the shame of his own failures.

At all points in the Compass of Shame there is damage to the person's ability to mature his feelings and feel at home with himself and others. Humility is the virtue that can heal our shame: we must allow ourselves to be loved and accepted with all our defects of character. This is what a twelve-step meeting offers people. The alcoholic, for example, fearfully attends his first AA meeting, probably threatened into attendance. He is full of shame and afraid of what others will think of him. But healing comes from a social situation because, as noted above, man was created in the image of God and God is not solitude enclosed upon itself but a Trinity of Persons. Healing comes, not from a one-to-one situation as much as from a fellowship of sufferers who can love the newcomer out of his shame. Love sets him free. It is important to bring wounded people into a fellowship of love, such as one finds in twelve-step programs (and is made evident for example in the closing remarks at an Alanon meeting, "After a while, you'll discover that though you may not like all of us, you'll love us in a very special way—the same way we already love you"). Belonging to an anonymous fellowship, the person feels accepted and has a sense of belonging that slowly begins to heal his shame. Finally, with St. Paul (2 Corinthians 12:9), he can boast of his weakness and announce, "Hi. My name is _____ and I'm an alcoholic." Shame free.

Pride, Humility, Self-loathing and Recovery

The Christian life is one of participating in the Eucharistic Mystery of Christ wherein He humbled Himself and gave us the supreme example of love. Pope Benedict teaches:

In this Easter mystery the Lord is inviting us to participate in His humility, that is, in His love for neighbor, so as to thus be participants in His glorification, making ourselves with Him into sons and daughters in the Son. Let us pray that the Lord helps us to conform ourselves to His humility, to His love, to thus be participants in His divinization.

The founders of AA knew that being ready to have one's defects of character removed was in direct proportion to one's humility. In order for God's grace to be fully operative in our lives, we must be fully open. It is humility that opens us by enabling us to see our defects at work to sabotage our happiness and to admit them to ourselves, God, and a sponsor. It is humility that allows us to love ourselves after a fall and keeps us from being scandalized that our weakness is weak, our infirmity infirm, and our frailty frail. Acknowledging ourselves as loved even though we are weak enables us to love our neighbors with the same love we see ourselves loved with. "Love your neighbor as yourself" (Mark 12:31) becomes possible with humility. Since Christian love must include love of God, of self, and of neighbor, we cannot love ourselves truly without loving God and our neighbor. We love ourselves when we love our neighbor, not only because it is our duty (fulfilling Christ's command), but also because it redounds to our good, since we are members of the same body. As St. Paul explains, "If one part suffers, all the parts suffer with it; if one part is honored, all the parts share its joy" (1 Corinthians 12:26). Loving our neighbor is the best way of loving ourselves, for it directs our focus away from ourselves, which is the cause of so much of our misery. The alcoholic learns to strengthen his recovery by reaching out to those who still suffer.

Litany of Humility

O Jesus, meek and humble of heart,
hear me.
From the desire of being esteemed,
deliver me.
From the desire of being extolled,
From the desire of being honored,
From the desire of being praised,
From the desire of being preferred to others,

From the desire of being consulted,
From the desire of being approved,
From the fear of being humiliated,
From the fear of being despised,
From the fear of being calumniated,
From the fear of being forgotten,
From the fear of being ridiculed,
From the fear of being wronged,
From the fear of being suspected,
That others may be loved more than I
Jesus, grant me the grace to desire it.
That others may be esteemed more than I,
That, in the opinion of the world,
others may increase and I may decrease,
That others may be chosen and I set aside,
That others may be praised and I go unnoticed,
That others may be preferred to me in everything,
That others may become holier than I,
provided that I may become as holy as I should.

Let us Pray.

O holy and most humble Savior Jesus, who, by Your example and by Your teachings, did command us to be meek and humble in imitation of Your incomparable gentleness and humility, be pleased to give me this grace, as You have given me the commandment. Enable me to do whatever You command, and command whatever

You desire. Destroy in me all proud thoughts and vain opinions of myself. I acknowledge to You that any worthwhile fruit from me, any good thing in me, comes from Your grace. I cannot boast, for what I have received from You is a gift. In relation to my fellow man, may I strive to honor others while giving You the glory. May I never seek my own praise, and may I never become puffed up when praise is offered to me. May I receive the honor, with which You will crown Your humble servants, in that kingdom where You live and reign for ever and ever. Amen.

Chapter Five

------◆------

Envy, Kindness, and Pusillanimity

> *Therefore, rid yourselves of all malice and all*
> *deceit, insincerity, envy, and all slander; like*
> *newborn babies, long for pure spiritual milk so*
> *that through it you may grow into salvation,*
> *for you have tasted that the Lord is good.*
>
> 1 Peter 2:1–3

Love is our salvation. St. Thomas Aquinas says of envy: "Envy according to the aspect of its object is contrary to charity's love, whence the soul derives its spiritual life…Charity rejoices in our neighbor's good, while envy grieves over it."[67] Envy, correctly understood, kills love. Some think envy is a feeling of jealousy for what others have. Rather, envy is sadness over our neighbor's good that is regarded as evil, inasmuch as it lessens our own excellence. I once heard a drug addict, in learning about someone's purchase of a beautiful new car, respond, "I hope he crashes it!" and taking great delight in the thought of that person's car being crashed—envy's secondary effect. There a connection in the drug addiction and the inability to rejoice in another's good. We can see this in the old Grimm Brothers' fairytale of *Snow White*.

The story relates that, once upon a time, as the queen sat sewing at her window, she pricked her finger with the needle and a drop of blood fell on the new snowfall on her windowpane. As she looked at the blood on the snow, she said to herself, "Oh, how I wish I had a daughter that had skin white as snow, lips red as blood, and hair black as ebony." Soon after that, the queen gave birth to a baby girl with skin white as snow, lips red as blood, and hair black as ebony. She named the princess Snow White. Shortly afterward, the queen died. Before long, however, the king took a new wife, who was quite beautiful but also very vain. The new queen possessed a magical mirror that would answer any question. She often asked: "Mirror, mirror on the wall, who in the land is the fairest of all?" to which the mirror always replied, "You, my queen, are fairest of all." But when Snow White reached the age of seven, she became more beautiful than her stepmother, and then, when the queen asked her mirror, it responded: "Queen, you are full fair, 'tis true, but Snow White is fairer than you." The queen became envious and ordered a huntsman to take Snow White into the woods to be killed. The queen regarded Snow White's beauty as a hindrance to her own. Her pride was hurt and she sought Snow White's destruction. We saw something similar in Olympic skater Tonya Harding's attack on her competitor Nancy Kerrigan, whom she perceived as a threat to her victory in the winter Olympics of 1994. She hired Shane Stant to break Kerrigan's right leg so that she would be unable to skate. Pride secretly fears all competition and dreads all rivals.

As these examples make evident, envy and pride are connected. The *Catechism* notes, "envy often comes from pride" (*CCC* #2540). St. Thomas explains why envy follows after pride: "[A]s a consequence [of pride], it was possible for envy also to be in [fallen angels], since to desire something involves resistance to anything contrary. Now the envious person is upset over the good possessed by another, inasmuch as he deems his neighbor's good to be a hindrance to his own…So, after the sin of pride, there followed the evil of envy in the sinning angel, whereby he grieved over man's good…" As with Snow White's stepmother, the devil grieved over man's good and sought to destroy it. Such is the nature of evil. Evil hates the good and seeks to pervert it. Likewise with beauty. We see this often in our society. For example, if a person drives his beautiful new car to the wrong section of town, there are those who would take great delight in scratching it. Satan was first proud, desiring to be the source of his own excellence, exempt from the grace of God. Then he became envious—envying God's greatness, and also envying the great dignity that God bestows upon man. Because of the power of evil, man needs God's grace to be victorious. Only He has the power to defeat evil. St. Thomas notes that through envy, the demons take a perverse pleasure in all sorts of human sins, insofar as these are hindrances to a man's good,[68] but this does not assuage their misery.

Envy is described as sadness over another's good that is regarded as an obstacle to one's personal advantage, as with Tonya Harding and Snow White's stepmother. Sometimes people will confess being envious, but in reality they mean "jealous" and even then, they are referring to a *feeling* of jealousy, wishing they had what someone else does. That is not envy as such. And remember, feelings in and of themselves are not sins.

Kindness: The Antidote

Knowing, then, that envy is a sin when purposefully indulged, acts of kindness are the antidote. Being good to those we are envious of and wishing them well, praying for their well-being and bearing them no ill will, coming to their aid in time of need is the way to defeat envy. The *Catechism* notes, "The sincere Christian struggles against envy by exercising good will. Since envy often comes from pride, further growth in the virtue of humility is required. If we want to see God glorified in us, then we must learn to rejoice in others' successes" (*CCC* #2540). This is an exercise in kindness, correctly understood. By kindness we mean promoting the good of another. St. Thérèse warns, "Do not allow kindness to degenerate into weakness," for on the opposite extreme from envy is pusillanimity. We don't often call someone pusillanimous in ordinary conversation, so let us use the adjective "spineless." Weak, spineless behavior can sometimes masquerade as kindness, but genuine kindness is no such thing. Rather, pusillanimity is often motivated by fear—fear of rejection, fear of displeasing, etc. True kindness seeks the good of others regardless of any return and irrespective of the recipient's attitude. A kind person can rejoice in the good of others while warding off feelings of resentment and sadness.

If envy is indulged, its offshoots can be: hatred, detraction, joy at another's misfortune and sadness at his success. A person envies someone toward whom he harbors ill will because of that person's success, achievement, etc. His self-worth depends on being better than another. He envies something that belongs to someone else and to which he is no right or claim. Notice that the envious person bears ill *will* toward another. The will must be involved for something to be a sin. Some people will confess envy, but when the priest questions them, it becomes clear there was no ill will involved but rather a feeling about another person—perhaps a feeling of sadness over another's good. That is not the deadly *sin* of envy. This misconception is often given in philosophical treatments of envy.[69] The truly envious person purposely nourishes the envy, and thus his will is involved in the sin of envy. But the feeling alone is no sin.

Envy, Kindness, Pusillanimity, and Recovery

Envy is a loser's game. Love is man's origin and love is his fulfillment. Envious behavior precludes love. As with all areas of twelve-step recovery, envy is a spiritual problem and calls for a spiritual solution. Recovery in Christian life cannot be deepened and fruitful unless a person seeks to overcome the capital vice of envy, for envious behavior betrays a lack of self-worth and self-acceptance that only sets a person up for addiction and codependency. A humble person accepts who he is and is happy about it, no matter what shortcomings he may possess or what others may have. We avail ourselves of God's unconditional love for us by offering His love back to him by loving others as He would have us. But this can't be done insofar as we allow ourselves to be victimized by nourishing envious behavior. Until a person can know himself as loved irrespective of any merits of his own, he is not free to love. Now addiction becomes the narcotic to dull the pain of self-loathing.

The appeal of Christianity is the appeal of truth, that while we were still sinners, Christ died for us, so much does God love us. All we need to do is embrace that unmerited love by offering it back to God by loving others. This is not possible if we harbor the deadly sin of envy. Working recovery issues in an anonymous fellowship wherein we can express ourselves freely and honestly without being shamed opens us to the grace of recovery. Not only do we no longer have to look good to others to feel good about ourselves, we no longer have to compare ourselves to others. Because we've begun to love ourselves just as we are, we can deal with any envious thoughts and desires by acts of kindness, irrespective of how we feel and thereby deepen our recovery. Acts of genuine kindness avoid spineless acts of weakness or pusillanimity. I once heard someone say that gentleness without honesty is nothing but sentimentality; and honesty without gentleness is nothing but brutality. In recovery, a person learns in meetings to speak openly and honestly, yet gently. The addict can be brutally honest. In his meetings when he begins to feel less threatened, he learns gentleness. The codependent can be gentle but not honest and suffers from the addict's brutality. In meetings, the codependent learns how to be honest. In recovery, true kindness, which defeats envy, is acquired.

Prayer for Kindness

Gentle Lord, make me generous in prosperity and thankful in adversity. I pray to be fair in judgment and guarded in speech. May I be a lamp to those who walk in darkness and a home to the stranger, eyes to the blind and a guiding light to the feet of the erring. Keep my heart open to the inspirations of the Your Spirit so that I may rejoice with those who rejoice and weep with those who weep. Lead me out of resentment to contentment, from anxiety to Your peace. I make this prayer through our Lord, Jesus Christ, Your Son, Who lives and reigns with You in the unity of the Holy Spirit, one God forever and ever. Amen.

Chapter Six

Avarice, Generosity, and Wastefulness

> *You covet but do not possess. You kill and envy*
> *but you cannot obtain; you fight and wage war.*
> *You do not possess because you do not ask.*
>
> James 4:2

In Shakespeare's *Macbeth*, Macbeth's tragic flaws were actually the deadly sins of avarice and envy. Macbeth is corrupted by his avarice for power and is willing to murder even friends if it means securing his position as king. Likewise is Lady Macbeth willing to risk anything for power. To see her husband king, she lies and kills and is eventually destroyed by her wickedness. The horror of avarice could not be better portrayed.

Avarice, or greed (from the Latin *avarus*, "greedy," "to crave"), is the inordinate desire for riches, whether material, spiritual, or artistic. Note the word "inordinate." It is a desire for the things of this world that is out of order, as when we place our desire for things before God and before our duty to family, etc. Note, too, that Scripture does not account money as the root of all evil, but rather the *love* of money: "For the love of money is the root of all of evils, and some people in their desire for it have strayed from the faith and have pierced themselves with many pains" (1 Timothy 6:10).

The special malice of avarice, broadly speaking, lies in that it makes the getting and keeping of money and possessions an end in itself. The avaricious person does not see that these things are valuable only as means to attain the goals for which God created him. These goods should be acquired according to a person's needs and with due regard for the special social condition in which he finds himself. Goods have been given us by God to be shared for love's sake. The avaricious person sins against this love.

Avaricious Behavior

As with the other deadly sins we've been considering, it is called a capital sin because it is the source from which other sins are committed. Contemporary culture gives plentiful evidence of avaricious behavior, the Ponzi scheme being just one of contemporary man's attempts at greed. This selfishness is portrayed in *The Life and Adventures of Martin Chuzzlewit* by Charles Dickens, which Dickens considered his best work. As seen in Dickens' story, avarice is more of a blanket term that can describe many other examples of greedy behavior. These include disloyalty; deliberate betrayal or treason, especially for personal gain, such as bribery; scavenging and hoarding of materials or objects; theft and robbery by means of violence;

trickery; and manipulation of authority. These are all actions that may be inspired by avarice. One has only to see the daily news to see the devastating effects of avaricious people and the untold harm it has brought their families.

Greed can disguise itself as a virtue under the pretext of providing for the future, whereby a person hoards things that are not really needed for his future well-being. Undue preoccupation with money and material things does not ordinarily become a mortal sin, but when money exerts such an attraction on people that they commit many sins for its sake, it becomes mortal. Such sins committed by the greedy are treachery, fraud, perjury, violence, and lack of mercy.

With regard to our current economic situation, we read in news reports:

The near collapse of our financial system in 2008 was driven by Wall Street executives whose obsession for ever-greater profits beyond all reason led to the creation of "derivatives" and other reckless financial instruments, incurring huge debt anchored by woefully inadequate reserves. This was facilitated by the complicity of successive Republican and Democratic congresses and administrations that, with flagrant lack of foresight, heedlessly relaxed our statutes governing oversight responsibilities. We think the central focus here was on greed.[70]

In our current economic collapse, we clearly see the devastating effects of greed. We read in Scripture that "it is easier for a camel to go through the eye of a needle than for one who is rich to enter the kingdom of God" (Mark 10:25).

One couldn't find a more extreme image for avarice than a camel going through the eye of a needle: totally impossible. What the Scripture stresses is that those who seek their security and salvation in money are doomed. The stock market crash of 1929 began a ten-year economic slump that affected all the Western industrialized countries. The decade that led up to the crash, the Roaring Twenties, was a time of wealth and excess. Despite caution of the dangers of speculation, many believed that the market could sustain high price levels. But it all came crashing down. And some wealthy people, who equated self-worth with net worth, committed suicide. Historian William K. Klingaman, who authored *1929: The Year of the Great Crash,* gives examples:

The wife of a Long Island broker shot herself in the heart; a utilities executive in Rochester, New York, shut himself in his bathroom and opened a wall jet of illuminating gas; a St. Louis broker swallowed poison; a Philadelphia financier shot himself in his athletic club; a divorcee in Allentown, Pennsylvania, closed the doors and windows of her home and turned on the gas oven. In Milwaukee, one gentleman who took his own life left a note that read: "My body should go to science, my soul to Andrew W. Mellon, and sympathy to my creditors."

The devil is crafty. Jesus calls him first a liar and then a murderer. A person first buys into the lie and then death follows (and here the death of our Christian culture). It is noteworthy that the nations with the highest GDP have the highest rates of mental illness, incarceration, divorce, and adultery, the United States having the highest.[71]

The attempt to ground one's security—one's salvation—in money is the evil, and not the riches themselves. St. Augustine made clear in his sermon on Lazarus and the rich man that the reason the rich man's soul was lost was not that he was rich—"after all, was not Lazarus greeted in heaven by a rich man—Abraham?!" Augustine warns against those who fail to distinguish between the rich and the avaricious. Often the envious disdain the rich and attempt to portray the successful as evil. There are wealthy people who, thanks to their wealth, have become benefactors to the poor, and great things have been achieved for the poor because of the generosity of the virtuous rich. For example, the many good works of Mother Teresa and her Missionaries of Charity are the result of the generosity of the wealthy. Generosity is the antidote to avarice.

On the other extreme is wastefulness, another defect of our hedonistic culture. It is reported that on average, U.S. households waste 14 percent of their food purchases. It is not uncommon in our land of plenty for people to take a few bites of something and toss the rest, to buy a product, never open it, and though still within the expiration date, toss it.[72] Denying ourselves for the benefit of those in need is called almsgiving, and it is part of Christian praxis. In this sense, a person's actions are realized in light of the way they affect those in need.

Avarice, Generosity, Wastefulness, and Recovery

As with Lady Macbeth, today's corporate world has shown itself to be plagued by avarice with its concomitant thirst for power. Corporate greed, with its excessive bonuses, has sown resentment in the American public. However, consumer greed is also to blame for contributing to the economic collapse, fueled by overspending and over-lending from banks. For example, in 2009 total household credit card debt was nearly $1 trillion.[73] As Christians, we need to avoid the allure of materialism that caters to waste and avarice in order to promote a culture of true generosity, not greed. Avarice is born of a person's insecurity. Instead of loving the other person, the avaricious person exploits him economically for his own advancement, setting his goal on this life alone. "You fool," Scripture says of the avaricious man, "this night your life will be demanded of you; and the things you have prepared, to whom will they belong?" (Luke 12:20). The anxiety and stress that come with avarice only encourage addiction and dependency. By using our blessings for the good of the poor and avoiding all waste, we strengthen our recovery.

Prayer for Generosity

Heavenly Father, teach me to be generous, to give and not count the cost. Though Your Son Jesus was rich, yet for my sake He become poor. He was made a curse that I might be blessed, He was wounded that I might be healed. Grant that covetousness of earthly goods may die in me, and the desire of heavenly things may live and grow in me. Keep me from all idle and vain expenditures that I may be a benefactor to those in need, and that giving not grudgingly nor of necessity, but cheerfully, I may come to new life in You, and be made through the merits of Your Son a partaker of the riches of Your heavenly treasure, You who live and reign forever and ever. Amen.

Chapter Seven

Anger, Patience and "Doormathood"

> *All bitterness, fury, anger, shouting, and reviling*
> *must be removed from you, along with all malice.*
> *Be kind to one another, compassionate, forgiving*
> *one another other as God has forgiven you in Christ.*
>
> Ephesians 4:31–32

The early desert monks relate a story about a fellow monk's gradual awareness of the true nature of his anger. The story goes that when he had finally had enough of those who caused his anger, he fled further out into the desert to live by himself in total isolation. This, he thought, would preserve his peace of soul and he would no longer have to live with anger. So he found himself a suitable cave and took up his eremitical life. Before long, however, his anger returned. One day he filled his terra-cotta mug with water, but it overturned and all its contents spilled out. Patiently he refilled it. But once again it tipped over. Trying to maintain his cool, he calmly walked to the cistern and refilled it a third time and a third time it tipped over. He flew into a rage, picked up the mug, and threw it, smashing against the wall of the cave. Later that evening at the time for prayer, feeling guilty, he prostrated before the Lord and repented of his anger. He recognized that the true battle of his anger lay within himself. He packed up his sparse belongings and returned to his companions. The real solution was the interior struggle against self. As with all sin, there is always present the primary sin of pride. Wounded egos need to take their anger out on others, for hurt people hurt other people and are easily slighted by others. Proverbs tells us, "Fools immediately show their anger, but the shrewd conceal contempt" (12:16). What should be a passion for justice often turns out to be a passion for vengeance because of egocentric self-interest. This is sinful anger.

Although anger is usually considered to be evil by its very nature, it is not. Not all anger is sinful. Individuals who have been hurt, betrayed, and abused have the right to be angry. Anger is an emotion and, as noted elsewhere, emotions have no moral value in and of themselves. St. Thomas Aquinas clearly teaches that the only evil to be found in anger is by reason of excess or defect.[74] As with all the moral virtues, the norm is guided by what is reasonable. It is easy to see that excessive anger or misdirected anger would be contrary to what is reasonable, but what is often not understood is that it could be morally evil not to be angry when circumstances reasonably demand it. Thus does St. Thomas distinguish between two distortions: excess and defect. If, for example, someone kidnaps and abuses your child but you are not spitting mad, something is emotionally wrong. You should be angry, and yet you should respond in a reasonable, responsible, and loving way in addressing the source of your anger. To this end, St. Thomas quotes St. John Chrysostom: "'He that is angry without cause, shall be in danger; but he that is angry with cause, shall not be in danger: for without anger, teaching will be useless, judgments unstable, crimes unchecked.' Therefore," St. Thomas adds, "to be angry is not always an evil."[75]

Anger can be good when we channel it to effect positive actions in our lives. Anger over injustices can lead us to advocate for changes in laws and policies, as with MADD. Candy Lightner founded the organization after her daughter, Cari, was killed by a drunk driver who was a repeat offender. Cindi Lamb joined with Candy after her own daughter became the nation's youngest quadriplegic at the hands of a drunk driver. These women channeled their anger into founding one of the most widely supported and well-liked nonprofit organizations in America, which has helped curb the evil of drunk driving. Their anger is praiseworthy, as St. Thomas notes, "But if one is angry in accordance with right reason, one's anger is deserving of praise." Anger can lead us to setting goals and taking steps to change behavior and better ourselves and others. Anger over mistakes can lead us to humility. Thus does St. Paul instruct, "Be angry but sin not" (Ephesians 4:26). We can see St. Paul's point in the life of our Lord. Because some people were abusing His Father's house, Jesus made a whip out of rope and in anger chased them out of the temple. St. Thomas notes that Jesus, in

His human nature, had a full complement of emotions—but without sin.

On the other hand, anger can become a catalyst for destructive behaviors that causes harm to ourselves and/or others. We are never angry unless someone has harmed us in some way (or we think they have). We thus lash out at the person we perceive as the cause of our distress.

Anger is no sin under three conditions:

1. if the cause of the anger is just;

2. if it is no greater than the cause demands;

3. if, once the action demanded by the situation is taken care of, we let go of the anger.

When we speak of anger as a deadly sin, we are concerned with unjust anger, i.e., anger that goes against the three principles enumerated above, meaning the anger is not justified, it is excessive, revengeful, and unreasonably out of control. The offspring of anger (those sins committed because of the anger) are: quarreling, being eager and quick to argue, cursing, indignation, and blasphemy. Thus anger sometimes leads to indignation, which is a feeling of hurt pride at having to endure some insult, or it may lead to unreasonable plotting and scheming, revenge against the person thought to be the cause of the hurt. Anger may lead to all kinds of actions that are contrary to Christian charity.

The Sin of Cruelty

Unjust anger can lead to cruel behavior. Cruelty can be defined as inflicting punishment that is unreasonable and unlawful. It manifests a hardness of heart and an inflexibility that is contrary to Christian mercy. Besides the mental attitude of cruelty, often the punishment given violates the law of justice. Thus a person is guilty of cruelty not only when he excessively punishes, but when he deliberately refuses to lessen the punishment that prudence deems right.

On the other hand, it would also be wrong for someone to excuse or lessen a punishment for a crime when the good of society demands that the evil be punished. Excessive laxity only rewards and encourages evil behavior and can also be an injustice to society. We often see this in today's society when a judge or jury or even a president pardons someone guilty of grave evils. St. Thérèse warns, "Do not allow kindness to degenerate into weakness."

Anger Healed

Christian behavior teaches against the anger that seeks to get even, for this anger only destroys civilized life. Thus did our Lord teach us to forgive our enemies. This is the hallmark of the Christian heart: forgiveness. Jesus taught us to pray in the Our Father, "forgive us our trespasses as we forgive those who trespass against us." We are to treat others as we would be treated. We have sinned; do we want those sins to be always held against us by God? No, we want mercy and forgiveness. In order to be forgiven, first we must forgive. The omnipotence of God, says St. Thomas, is shown, above all in the act of his forgiveness and the use of his mercy, for the way He has of showing his supreme power is to pardon freely.[76] Nothing makes us so Godlike, notes St. John Chrysostom, as the willingness to forgive.[77] We can assuage our anger by lowering our expectations and not expecting things to go our way. Often the angry, impatient person is living in an illusion of there being such a thing as a normal situation exempt from difficulty. The patient person accepts reality: it's an imperfect world that doesn't revolve around me and the way I think things should be. Seen this way, I can forgive.

Forgiveness, however, is not a feeling. Some people will say to the priest, "Father, I can't forgive," whereby they mean that they cannot remove the feeling of anger against those who inflicted an injustice. Or they think that to forgive means that they have to approve of the evil done against them. No. Forgiveness is not simply about feelings (just as love and sin are not simply about feelings). Anger is a feeling. It is has no moral value in and of itself. But if we respond to our anger excessively, if we allow our anger to make our decisions for us, instead of doing what is reasonable, then sin enters in. To forgive is to pray for the evildoer, to bear him no ill will, to want what is good for that person, to pray for his conversion, etc. There is no moral obligation to like the person, nor do we have to have anything to do with the evildoer if he is a danger. The meek and patient person bears no ill will and is ready to forgive. As Aristotle says, the "good-tempered man is not disposed to take vengeance but rather to pardon."[78] The virtue is to be "angry" in the right way, at the right time. We should not leap to vengeance. As St. Thomas comments, "When we call a person meek, we signify that he is not inclined to punish but to forgive and remit punishments."[79] Being good-tempered or meek is a moral virtue having to do with a mean between extremes: the extremes of wrath and "doormathood."[80] Patience enables the possibility of love between us, but it does not mean tolerating intolerable behavior, something from which the "doormat" needs to recover.

Patience stands between wrath and "doormathood." Some people think that "to turn the other cheek" (cf. Matthew 5:38–42) means having to tolerate intolerable behavior, to let people walk all over you. Saint Augustine remarks, "Who is our primary example of the Christian life? Jesus. What did Jesus do when He was struck across the face? He answered, 'Why do you strike Me?'" St. Augustine notes that Jesus did not offer the other side of His face to be struck (cf. John 18: 19–34). Augustine notices the same behavior in St. Paul. When Paul was struck across the face, he responded in anger, saying, "God will strike you, you white-washed wall" (cf. Acts 23:3). Augustine teaches that turning the other cheek is a phrase in Christian doctrine that refers to responding to an aggressor without violence.[81] It means never returning evil for evil. But it certainly does not mean remaining silent in the face of injustice. We have a right to be angry when there is injustice, but our anger must be directed toward the injustice and not in excess by delighting in hurting the other.

Forgiveness allows for the punishment of the evildoer. St. Augustine argues that punishment is in harmony with the teaching of Christ when it fulfills two criteria. First, it must be aimed at correction. Punishment is an act of mercy, he says, when it has this goal in mind. Second, punishment is acceptable when the Christian has overcome the natural hatred that accompanies the desire for vengeance. In this, Augustine refers to Scripture's claim that the Lord chastens those whom he loves (Hebrews 12:6).[82] This is a model for the Christian use of punishment.

Anger, Patience, Doormathood, and Recovery

Anger is a major issue with addicted personalities and codependents. They often harbor a lot of anger that has never been honestly addressed. Being insensitive to our feelings and emotions is a vice. Anger needs to be acknowledged and processed even though most people are not comfortable with their anger, especially those who've grown up in emotionally oppressive environments, as seen in the following statement by a man about his brother's untimely death:

Right after I got out of Harvard, my younger brother— whose passage into adulthood had been even more troubled than my own—had fallen off a Boston boat and drowned. A lengthy autopsy revealed what I could have told anyone if they'd asked: that my brother had been a habitual user of alcohol and morphine…The funeral that followed was full of respectful but perfectly nonsensical tributes, all of which avoided the subject of my brother's adult battle with terrible bouts of depression. There were many causes of his unhappiness, but at heart I believe now, as I believed then, that it was essentially the result of growing up in a household, and a world, where emotional expression of any kind was at best frowned upon and at worst strangled.[83]

Anger that is not dealt with in a healthy way but is suppressed and turned inward often leads to depression. We need to admit our anger and deal with it in a reasonable, responsible, and loving way. This is done by taking an inventory of one's anger. Where is it coming from? Perhaps our expectations are too high—an expectation is a premeditated resentment—and we need to lower our expectations. With that our anger dissipates. Anger over things we have no control of is a worthless loss of energy. We can tell ourselves, "Let go and let God." It is also good to remember AA's maxim: hurt people hurt people. We can show some compassion or, as Mother Teresa puts it, "understanding love." As with all the passions, anger is meant for love's sake. Christian charity is a participation in God's love for another. With grace we come to have God's interest in the other person. Anger is assuaged by doing the right thing with loving patience and forgiveness.

Prayer for Patience

Lord, as You have dealt gently and patiently with me, help me to be gentle and patient in all the events of my life: in disappointments, in the thoughtlessness of others, in the insincerity of those I trusted, in the unfaithfulness of those upon whom I relied. Let me never be so self-concerned that I neglect to enjoy the happiness of others. May my struggles, pains, and heartaches teach me patience and help me grow closer to You. May my wounds be sacred, like Yours, and not bitter. May the understanding love You teach in Your passion make me broad in my forgiveness, not narrow or proud. May no one be less good for having come within my influence; no one less pure, less true, less kind, less noble, for having been a fellow traveler with me in this pilgrimage of life. When trouble afflicts me, may I love You anyway, as You loved from the cross. May my life be lived in the radiance of Your presence with my heart set on the life that will never end and so be eternally happy with You who live and reign for ever and ever. Amen.

Chapter Eight

Sloth, Diligence, and Workaholism

I passed by the field of the slothful, by the vineyard of one with no sense. It was all overgrown with thistles; its surface was covered with nettles, and its stone wall broken down.

Proverbs 24:30–31

Our moral life involves acquiring good habits called virtues. Because virtues are good habits, they dispose us toward good actions. We act in accord with our dispositions, and thus the importance of acquiring good habits to combat the pull of the seven deadly sins. Our psychological well-being is bolstered by building virtues. With strong virtues, a person is able to do the right thing despite the difficulties involved and how he feels about it. As with the other deadly sins, sloth destroys love. In everyday parlance, sloth is considered simple physical laziness, whereas in traditional Christian moral teaching, it is something far deeper than mere laziness. It comes from a root Greek word meaning "negligence."

I recently attended a funeral of a woman who died suddenly from pancreatic cancer. She was only seventy-two. In the pamphlet handed out at the funeral, she was described as follows:

She loved life, her faith, her family, and friends. Whatever she did she always succeeded. There was always a goal for her, right up until the end of her life. She never knew a stranger...

This woman's life was the opposite of that of the slothful. She used the time given her to be creative and successful, so great was her love of life, of God, and of her family.

The Hopelessness of Sloth

Sloth has to do with giving into hopelessness and loss of meaning, which can manifest itself in a lack of concern for the well-being of others. St. Thomas emphasizes sloth's unhappiness with the demands of love. Because he gives into an oppressive sorrow, the slothful person wants to do nothing. He simply indulges this sorrow in a life that neglects the pursuit of goodness. According to St. Thomas, the root of despair is to be found in sloth, wherein a person fails to believe in God's loving concern about him. Sloth can so oppress a person that he neglects his duties and fails to seek God's will in his life. Sloth is one of the ways we can sin against God's love because it goes so far as to refuse the joy that comes from God and to be repelled by the goodness and even the grace of God.

How does one overcome sloth? With the grace of God made available and accepted in a genuine spiritual life, we begin to stimulate our hearts for a love of genuine goodness. One cannot attain the virtue of diligence without a desire for it. So if the slothful person is lacking in desire, his first step is to increase his desire to live a spiritual life. How does one go about this? By reading good literature and watching good documentaries, biographies, and movies that stimulate a person to want to better live a Christ-centered life. Another is to consider the great evils we see in the news and to ask ourselves, "Do I want to contribute to the sum total of evil in the world or the sum total of goodness?" Contemplating the horrors of such great evil can stimulate the heart to want great goodness, and one sets off on the road of diligence, struggling against sloth. Sloth is a loss of spiritual moorings in life, and so, as with the recovering alcoholic, one needs to be committed to an apostolate: as the recovering alcoholic reaches out to someone who still suffers, so too must the slothful commit to finding meaning in life by helping others. Doing good is self rewarding.

The other extreme of the virtue of diligence is workaholism. Someone defined the workaholic as one who regards work as more fun than fun. It is not to be confused with working hard; rather, the workaholic is addicted to work, which often masks a deeper fear of failure. Anytime we go too far in anything in a compulsive way, repeating a behavior despite negative consequences, it is an addiction. A person becomes dependent on it in ways that detract from other responsibilities, such as being with family, taking care of the home, watching over and relating to one's children. The workaholic avoids fun perhaps because fun is beyond his control, as with Captain von Trapp in the musical production of *The Sound of Music*. He couldn't even bear having his children wear playclothes. The workaholic is more involved with his work than with his family and friends and is obsessed with his work to the point of always being preoccupied with it. Even the Lord took time away from others to be with his closest disciples. He withdraws with them to a peaceful place (Luke 5:16; cf. Mark 1:35). This is an important exercise for the workaholic. It is important for the workaholic to nourish his spiritual life and diligently give time to things other than work, seeking a balance in his life.

Sloth, Diligence, Workaholism, and Recovery
Workaholism is just as much a vice as sloth. Because there's less of a social stigma attached to workaholism than to other addictions, the problem can easily go unrecognized, especially by the workaholic. But his friends and family often recognize the problem because the workaholic seems more interested in his work than in them. Often fearing failure, the workaholic derives his identity and self-worth from what he does, to the point of neglecting his health, relationships, and spiritual life. Japan has come to recognize workaholism as a serious issue among its citizens. Just as the United States has coined the term "workaholic" to give a name to this vice, so Japan has coined the term *karōshi* since it now considers workaholism a serious social problem leading to early death, often on the job. Overwork was popularly blamed for the fatal stroke of Japan's Prime Minister Keizo Obuchi at the age of sixty-three.

As with other addictions, the workaholic is in denial and simply thinks he needs to work hard. But any time we go too far with anything, our actions are disordered. Thus a person can be a workaholic in hobbies, exercise, housework, volunteering, or in trying to save the world. It can affect even friars, monks, and nuns who immerse themselves in work with little time for spiritual exercises. Recovery from workaholism and sloth takes diligence, a virtue that can be acquired with the help of twelve-step recovery, where a person learns to take time for his spiritual health and well-being while relating honestly to others in an anonymous fellowship. There he can absorb the spiritual principles of the steps and, with the help of a sponsor, find sobriety to live a balanced life.

Prayer for Diligence

Father in heaven, You made Jesus our model of love. You have made all the commandments of the law to enable me to love You and my neighbor. Grant that I may love You with all my heart, with all my mind, and all my soul, and love my neighbor for Your sake. Instill in me the grace of perseverence and that apathy may die in me. Fill my heart with understanding love, so that by constantly seeking to grow spiritually while seeking the happiness and success of others, I may follow You in the journey of faith with true and perfect love. Amen.

Chapter Nine

Gluttony, Temperance, and Deficiency

> *Their end is destruction, their god is their belly, and they glory in their shame, with minds set on earthly things.*
>
> Philippians 3:19

An ever-present preoccupation in today's media is the subject of obesity. We are an obese nation with increasing risks in diabetes. The nation's $40 billion diet industry sells outrageously expensive surgical procedures and drugs that have done little, if anything, to trim America's ever-growing collective waistline. Who is at the greatest risk for diabetes? Overweight people. Roughly 17 million Americans suffer from diabetes, of which gluttony is a major cause. Most medical problems suffered by overweight Americans are caused by poor nutrition and deplorable eating habits. The high cost of gluttony is financial as well as life-threatening. In 2001, about

295,000 people died in the United States from obesity-related illnesses at an estimated cost of $117 billion in health care. Sadly, for the first time in the history of earth, obesity is a problem for children and is reaching epidemic rates in the United States.[84] But not only is overeating a serious health issue, so also is its opposite—the undernourished bulimic and anorexic.

Feasting and Fasting

Traditionally the Christian life has been one of both fasting and feasting. Today's culture, however, knows little about fasting and self-denial. Modern secular culture greatly influences the day-to-day life of the Christian. Although my father was an atheist, he very much was a Christian in many respects. This is true because he was born in 1905 when American culture was formed by Christian mores. It's a given that culture powerfully influences thoughts, emotions, and behaviors. In fact, culture is an important part of our formation. We are social beings by nature, and culture impacts our standard rules of thought, emotion, and behavior. Our socialization occurs in a context, that context we call culture. It definitely shapes our perceptions.

Because of the pervasive reality of media outlets such as movies, music, television, video games, Internet, and magazines—all readily available on one's cell phone—now more so than any other time in American history, we are influenced by popular culture. Today's pop culture influences how we live and think, both positively and negatively. Whether it is a positive or negative effect, it is a reality we must be aware of and inventory from time to time. Culture can do much to change attitudes, as it has been doing with smoking, for example. The media could be a great help in reforming people's habits. Fasting, however, is not something that the media understands or values, except perhaps for vanity's sake. The Christian life is one of fasting because our human nature, wounded and weakened by original and personal sin, needs to be strengthened in order to gain victory over the poisonous stimuli that surround us. Abstinence is actually a virtue Christians are called to acquire. In countering those who say that it is not a virtue, St. Thomas responds with a quote from Scripture:

> **It is written (2 Peter 1:5–6): "Join with your faith virtue, and with virtue knowledge, and with knowledge abstinence"; where abstinence is numbered among other virtues. Therefore abstinence is a virtue.**[85]

And to those who would argue that gluttony is not a sin, St. Thomas responds:

> **I answer that, gluttony denotes, not any desire of eating and drinking, but an inordinate desire. Now desire is said to be inordinate through leaving the order of reason, wherein the good of moral virtue consists: and a thing is said to be a sin through being contrary to virtue. Wherefore it is evident that gluttony is a sin.**[86]

Sin is a mixture of the good and the bad. The desire for food and drink is not only natural and good, but in fact must be acted upon if we are to continue to live. It becomes sinful when, as St. Thomas notes above, we go too far, contrary to what is reasonable, by consuming excessive quantities of food, by consuming foods that deprive the body of the nourishment it needs in a balanced diet, or by eating too often.

Monastic communities traditionally have a very moderate diet. It is interesting that modern society sees a connection between too much red meat and cancer, too much fat in the diet and heart decease. These were the same foods that figured in the monastic fast, with the exception being that the monks, in contrast to modern society, saw a spiritual connection. Monks knew from experience that there is a connection between rich foods and the excitement of the passions. Their fast consisted primarily of substantial bread, vegetables, herbs, and beans. Feasting was done on special Christian feasts.

The Christian life is also one of feasting because as Christians we are called to appreciate God's bountiful providence and celebrate various feasts in regard to the life of Christ and of the saints. Typically, Christians would fast before the major feast day of a favorite saint, and on the saint's feast day, celebrate with great solemnity. Down through the centuries fasting and feasting have been integral parts in Christian living. Gluttony, coming from the Latin *gluttire*, meaning to gulp down or swallow, refers to excessive indulgence in food or drink. The moral deformity discernible in this vice lies in its defiance of the order given by reason, which prescribes necessity as the measure of indulgence in eating and drinking. All sin is contrary to right reason. Gluttony is disordered eating and drinking. This disorder, according to Saint Thomas, may happen in five ways: too soon, too expensively, too much, too eagerly, too fastidiously.[87] Clearly one who uses food or drink in such a way, gravely injuring his health or impairing the mental abilities needed for fulfilling his duties, is guilty of the sin of gluttony. To eat or drink exclusively for the mere pleasure of the experience is likewise gluttony.

As we have noted, in traditional moral theology the seven deadly sins are said to have offspring, i.e., behaviors that the deadly sins propagate. They beget other sins that flow from them. Each of the seven deadly sins has certain sins related to it and often committed because of it. Those of gluttony are said to be mental dullness, talkativeness, coarseness, vulgarity, impurity, and ridiculous behavior.

Gluttony is, in general, a venial sin in so far as it is an undue indulgence in a thing that is in itself neither good nor bad. Of course it is obvious that a different estimate would have to be given of one so wedded to the pleasures of the table as to absolutely and without qualification live merely to eat and drink, one of the number of those, described by the apostle St. Paul, "whose god is their belly." Such a one would be guilty of mortal sin if it interfered with one's major responsibilities or seriously harmed one's health. Moreover, a person who, by excesses in eating and drinking, would have greatly impaired his health, or became unfit for carrying out his obligations, would be justly chargeable with mortal sin. Contained here is the notion that overindulgence weighs down the spirit. It is also connected with our relationship to the poor, who do not have proper food. St. Augustine connects fasting to the law of love wherein he sees the poor one as Christ Himself. He says:

Above all remember the poor, so that what you withhold from yourselves by living more sparingly, you may deposit in the treasury of heaven. Let the hungry Christ receive what the fasting Christian receives less of. Let the self-denial of one who undertakes it willingly become the support of the one who has nothing. Let the voluntary want of the person who has plenty become the needed plenty of the person in want.[88]

St. Paul equates gluttony with idolatry, for any time we place something before God and in place of God, it is indeed idolatry. He warns, "For many, as I have often told you and now tell you even in tears, conduct themselves as enemies of the cross of Christ. Their end is destruction. Their God is their stomach; their glory is in their 'shame.' Their minds are occupied with earthly things" (Philippians 3:18–19). Every Christian is called to the cross of a sharing-sparing lifestyle inspired by the life of Christ and His saints. Exercising the virtue of temperance is a daily exercise in love, for love puts God first. We have a moral obligation to care for the temple of our bodies (cf. I Corinthians 6:19).

As with alcohol addiction, food addiction can be aided by a community of recovery, for example Overeaters Anonymous encourages twelve-step spirituality for compulsive eaters. Often a person is not aware of what triggers his addiction, but an anonymous fellowship of recoverers aids in enlightening a person. OA is not a weight-loss program. Rather, it addresses the physical, emotional, and spiritual aspects of the addict's life and brings healing in these areas.

The opposite extreme is insensibility. St. Thomas explains that God has placed pleasure in the operations that are necessary for man's life. Making use of these pleasures is no sin provided they are used according to reason. He says: "Now nature has introduced pleasure into the operations that are necessary for man's life. Wherefore the natural order requires that man should make use of these pleasures, insofar as they are necessary for man's well-being, as regards the preservation either of the individual or of the species. Accordingly, if anyone were to reject pleasure to the extent of omitting things that are necessary for nature's preservation, he would sin, as acting counter to the order of nature. And this pertains to the vice of insensibility."[89] However, St. Thomas also notes that it is sometimes praiseworthy and even necessary to abstain from such pleasures, as when athletes or soldiers deny themselves for a greater good.

The other extreme is those who starve themselves for various reasons. Lacking a balance in their lives, these people with an obsessive fear of gaining weight are unable to maintain a healthy body weight. As with all the vices, there is a connection with a distorted self-image. It has the highest mortality rate of any psychiatric disorder. It occurs most often in women but is found in men as well. I once met a father with a strong desire to live vicariously through his son. He pressured his son into being a football hero. Finally, the son become so anorexic that he was at the point of dying. Even knowing this, the father still had trouble refraining from pushing his son to do something he wasn't happy doing.

Similar to anorexia is bulimia. Bulimia is an illness in which a person binges on food or has regular episodes of overeating and feels a loss of control. The affected person then uses various methods—such as vomiting or laxative abuse—to prevent weight gain.

Gluttony, Temperance, Deficiency, and Recovery

The prevalence of these illnesses in a culture that has lost all operative understanding of the role of virtue in the character formation of the human person is only too understandable. Temperance needs to be taught by example, starting at home when the child is being trained in good habits. Sadly the culture is of no help, at least not as things are now. If only the culture could do for temperance in food and drink what it has done with its campaign against smoking, we could be hopeful for the well-being of our citizens. The culture should promote healthy, virtuous behavior and not prey upon people's weaknesses. Sadly, such is not the case, but certainly Christian families, churches, and schools should promote temperance. God is so powerful He can bring good out of anything, and so it can be for those suffering from the enemies of temperance. I once replied to the recovering alcoholic who urged me to learn the wisdom of the steps, "Toni, I'm glad you're an alcoholic!" And I said this because if it weren't for her own growth in wisdom that gave witness to the power of the steps, I would not have developed this ministry. God would never allow anything to happen in the past that's not part of His loving plan for the future. By cooperating with His grace and growing in temperance, we free ourselves from those obstacles to love.

Prayer for Temperance

Father, through Your Son, our Lord Jesus Christ, You have given us an example of self-denial. Through the grace of Christ, our bread of life and the mirror of abstinence, Who fasted forty days and forty nights, grant that, in serving You and not my own desires, I may live soberly and piously with contentment, without avarice, gluttony, or drunkenness. Give me, O Lord, an ever-watchful heart that no unworthy affection can draw away from You, a heart that no tribulation can crush, a heart that no temptation can warp. Make me truthful without disguise, given to good works without grumbling, faithful in correcting serious rongs without arrogance, and every ready to edify by word and example without pretense. Through Your grace may I always hunger and thirst for goodness, and find in Christ, the bread of life, all that my heart desires. Amen.

Chapter Ten

Lust, Chastity and Prudishness

> *Therefore, sin must not reign over your mortal bodies so that you obey their desires. And do not present the parts of your bodies to sin as weapons of wickedness, but present yourselves to God as raised from the dead to life and the parts of your bodies to God as weapons for righteousness.*
>
> Romans 6:12–13

The biblical story of Susanna and the two elders (Daniel 13:1–64) is a classic tale of unrequited lust. Two men plot the seduction of the beautiful Susanna after hiding in her private garden to watch her bathe. Inflamed by the sight of her naked body, they surprise her and tell her they will accuse her of meeting a young man if she does not consent to lie with them. She refuses to be blackmailed and is arrested and about to be put to death for promiscuity when a young man named Daniel interrupts the proceedings, demanding that the elders be questioned. After being separated, the two men are questioned about the details of what they saw. Their story doesn't square and thus their lie is made known and they—instead of Susanna—are put to death.

Lust is considered a deadly sin in all three of the world's monotheistic religions, for it perverts man's natural desire for union with a spouse. Just as God has created us with a desire for food that gives us pleasure while it sustains our life, so we are designed to take pleasure in acts of intimacy with a spouse that strengthens martial unity and preserves the human race. This pleasure is permissible to married people, provided they use it for these purposes. Otherwise, it is a sin against the sixth and ninth commandments (Exodus 20:14, 17). Unlike true intimacy, lust reduces another person to a mere object and is involved in a kind of destruction. Alternatively, a person who allows himself to be used is involved in a kind of suicide. In neither case is love the operative principle.

What is Lust?

Lust is an inordinate desire for sexual pleasure. Inordinate means "out of order." When we divert anything from the purpose for which it was intended by God, it is disordered. The malice of lust consists in an excessive attachment to sexual pleasure for the married, or the deliberate indulgence of sexual acts and pleasures for those who are unmarried. Just as considerable evidence indicates that most alcoholics inherit strong genetic propensity toward alcohol addiction, so too are findings with regard to lust and other addictions.

Lust is one of the seven deadly sins because it is so alluring that people will commit a wide variety of sins because of it. When a person is lost to lust, the faculties of his soul—the intellect and the will—become disordered in the following ways:

- Regarding the intellect, man's understanding, which should tell him whether or not something is good and therefore should be pursued, is afflicted by blindness that closes the mind to every good except sexual pleasure. People often wonder how a grown man could sexually abuse a child, but lust (as with all serious sin) darkens the intellect and keeps the lust addict in denial about the seriousness of his sexual sin.

- The act of judgment is upset by thoughtlessness whereby a person excludes any means to do what has to be done except those that lead to sexual pleasure. Thus a lust addict might neglect his duties toward his family in pursuit of acting out sexually, all the while denying the negative impact this behavior has on his wife and children. When a person is blinded by lust, he sees no evil.

- Regarding the will, lust results in inordinate self-love because of catering to one's disordered passions, which eventually tend toward a rejection of God or the Church, both of which are regarded as obstacles to one's self-indulgence. Secondly, lust results in inordinate attachment to this world, which often leads a person to despair of the world to come.

A dose of the daily news too often shows how lust can destroy a person's humanity and reduce him to the level of an animal. We speak of "man's inhumanity to man." Monstrous acts have been committed by those who have surrendered themselves to this deadly sin. A person can be so addicted to lust that it totally blinds him to the heinousness of his actions. It should be obvious, however, that a person does not start out lusting in so monstrous a fashion. Lust begins in the heart.

Internal Acts of Lust

It is not merely exterior actions that are prohibited, for Jesus warned, "I say to you, everyone who looks at a woman with lust, has already committed adultery with her in his heart" (Matthew 5:28). Thus, interior human and deliberate acts such as fantasies, thoughts, desires, etc. accepted and enjoyed are prohibited. Internal acts of lust are thoughts or desires that are not carried out in act. These are forbidden by the ninth commandment. External acts of lust are unchaste or impure deeds and words; these are also forbidden by the sixth commandment. A Christian avoids impure thoughts not only because they are evil in themselves, but also because all impure actions begin in the mind. A disciplined body comes from a disciplined mind. As one of the deadly sins, lust is something most individuals have to come to grips with.

Escape From Reality

Finding life in this valley of tears unbearable, people are often tempted to resort to all kinds of escapes. When a young person isn't taught how to deal with reality in a healthy way, he searches for something that seems to bring relief and comfort, something that is reliable and always there. As we have already seen, this may be alcohol or drugs, for others it may be food, and for others, there is sexual gratification. Such a person uses sex to medicate bad feelings. Some people discover early in life that sexual arousal can be a pleasant "drug" used in order to "medicate" themselves and to escape reality. Once indulged, it becomes an immediate addiction for many, especially for young males. Sex becomes confused with comfort and nurture. If a person marries without having overcome the addiction to lust, an unhappy sexual relationship often results. The person tends to use the spouse for his own gratification purely and simply. Ultimately this alienates them instead of strengthening their bond. Lust precludes intimacy, whereas genuine intimacy strengthens the bond of love.

Some Examples

- A young man had a problem of lust through the use of pornography and masturbation, with periodic visits to a strip joint. When confronted with his lust addiction, he quickly responded, "But I'm getting married!" He thought, "I won't need porn or strip joints; I'll have my wife." And he was most serious. Unfortunately, lust in marriage is never seen as an evil by the lust addict, and equally unfortunate is the fact that many spouses of lust addicts think that indulging their sexual fantasies is legitimate, even though their gut reaction may be one of disgust.

- A young woman asked to see the priest after Mass one evening. Married for only a year, she didn't really want to go home. She'd recently had a miscarriage and needed to abstain from sexual intercourse for a while. The problem was, her husband wouldn't hear of it. He wanted his fix, and if she didn't cooperate, he would use it against her. "Sounds like your husband has a lust problem," the priest responded. The next week she returned to speak again with the priest and admitted that she had lived with the man for five years before they decided to marry. Reflecting on those five years, she said, "I never really did like sex." What she wasn't aware of is that most people involved with lust addicts don't enjoy sex either, because having sex with the addict is simply being used and it most often feels dirty. It is not true intimacy; lust precludes intimacy.

- Another woman reported being very uncomfortable because her husband demanded very bizarre sexual acts that grossed her out. When she was told that her husband possibly had a sex addiction, her response was typical of an enabler, "I only wanted to please him." The next day her husband came to see the priest. He admitted that he had been seeing prostitutes. His poor wife had no clue, nor did she realize she was setting him up to increase his dose—a codependent sexual relationship.

- Recently a man returned to his Catholic faith at the age of thirty-four. He spoke of his sexual addiction—a life of sex with women, pornography, and masturbation.

But in returning to the Church, he reformed. However, he was still masturbating. While visiting a friend from high school, he picked up his friend's sweet little daughter and held her on his lap. He became sexually aroused and was even tempted by her. He asked the priest, "What am I now, a pedophile?"

In reading the saints and doctors of the Church, one doesn't hear of bisexuality, pedophilia, ephebophilia, or homosexuality. It is prudent to stay away from secular arguments dealing with these issues and deal simply with the real issue: a lack of sexual sobriety. All people, married or single, are called to a life of purity in mind and body. Why? Because man was created as a social being to exist in relationships with other people in love. Love is our origin and love is our fulfillment. Lust, however, disturbs our relationships and distorts true love. It prohibits true intimacy in marriage and keeps unmarried people from the intimate joy of nonsexual bonding. If a male is drawn to another male in affection, is that wrong? If the man mentioned above is drawn to his best friend's daughter, is that wrong? A young child should be a delight to the soul; to hold her is the delight of human affection. But for the man with a lust problem, a man who has never recovered from the habit of masturbation, such an attraction can become sexualized, whether the affective attraction is for the same sex, the opposite sex, or the child. This is the origin of pedophilia, ephebophilia, bisexuality, homosexuality, and sexual abuse in marriage: a lack of chastity or sexual sobriety.

It may happen that a young boy loses his father at an early age and, unfortunately, never has the opportunity to bond with a father figure. Seeking comfort in masturbation as a teenager, and still hungry for a father's love and attention, he gets his wires crossed, so to speak, and sexualizes his legitimate need for male attention and affection. Someone else can have a natural attraction to children, a veritable pied piper. There is nothing wrong with this ability to relate to children and enjoy their company, but if the person has a compulsive lust problem, then chances are he is going to sexualize the attraction. It is the same in marriage.

The young man referred to above, who is about to get married but is still masturbating and using pornography, is not wrong in seeking marriage. The problem, however, is his lust addiction: he is really not yet capable of intimacy, for lust precludes intimacy. Studies have shown that repeated exposure to pornography results in a decreased satisfaction with one's sexual partner and, like alcohol addiction, a person's tolerance level changes. The lust addict uses the partner for his own sexual gratification, whereas in a true Christian union, one gives oneself unreservedly to the spouse in true intimacy and, in the giving, receives. True intimacy strengthens the marriage bond.

Artificial Birth Control

The use of artificial birth control often promotes sex as a drug. Sex becomes a habit, and a habit becomes a need. The person needs a fix; sex is the needle in the arm. If a person who uses sex as a drug, that is, out of a compulsive need rather than a loving union, has to delay gratification, as he would if he were practicing natural birth control, he risks becoming irritable and unreasonable—as with the man mentioned above married to the woman who "never liked sex." Unreasonable demands are often placed on the marriage partner by a person with little or no sexual sobriety. Blind to his lust addiction, he fails to understand the emotional dependency that often underlies the sexual. Marriage without sexual sobriety yields to control, expectations, and need.

The ideologically tinted media is so ready to condemn the Church and make her appear irrelevant by quoting those Catholics who reject the Church's teaching on artificial birth control. Never heard are the stories of those Christians (Catholics and Protestants alike) who practiced birth control and saw the damaging effects it had on their marriages and on true intimacy. But the priest meets these people in parish after parish. Through experience, these couples have had the grace to recognize the deadly sin of lust in their marriage, something the worldly man or woman thinks an absurdity. Americans have witnessed the spouse of a sex addict travel as a political agent of her government throughout the world encouraging the use of birth control and abortion, all the while married to an unrecovered sex addict. What good is his use of birth control going to do to the women he has seduced? Wouldn't the self-control that comes with the virtue of chastity not only benefit his marriage but his relationship with all women? The institutionalization of sex is something the Church struggles against; but because of that, the Church is portrayed as the enemy, while at the same time she is portrayed as the enemy in harboring sex offenders, bringing to mind Jesus' remark: "They are like children who sit in the marketplace and call to one another, 'We played the flute for you, and you did not dance. We sang a dirge, but you did not weep'" (Luke 7:32). The people responded neither to John the Baptist, who "neither eating food nor drinking wine" and they said he was possessed nor Jesus "who came eating and drinking" and they called him a glutton. They rejected both messages and criticized those who brought the message. Today, the Church—like John the Baptist—is a voice crying in the wilderness, while society experiences more and more the devastating effects of a culture addicted to lust. The Church is criticized both for its message of chastity and for having clergy who have betrayed chastity!

The deadliness of the sin of lust can be demonstrated by the statistics. It is said that one in ten middle-aged women has been sexually abused as a child, that one in five children, from kindergarten to high school, has been sexually molested. If true, such statistics reinforce what is implied from the mass media: an enormous amount of sexual abuse is taking place in our contemporary culture. The culture has lost all operative understanding of true sexual intimacy.

Sexual addiction is becoming evermore institutionalized despite the statistical warning. Sex is used to sell everything, and rare is the movie that does not depict lust in a favorable light, whether between the married or unmarried, the same sex or the opposite sex. And now our young, in being encouraged to use condoms at increasingly younger ages, are being given the not-so-subtle message that sex outside of marriage is practically unavoidable. And women, so long victims of sexual abuse, are actually promoting it by encouraging their daughters to act out by encouraging "protection" instead of forming them to find men whose interest in them transcends the sexual.

Adults enable this behavior by saying, "They'll do it anyway." In reality, if advertisement against smoking works, why wouldn't it work against the abuse of sex? Is it because adults in our society are unwilling to give up the drug of lust themselves, just as we are unwilling to deny the eating and drinking habits that have resulted in a nation where obesity is a major health problem? There is no way to escape the need for self-denial and delayed gratification.

Nonsexual Bonding

It is not uncommon to meet young adults who have never experienced the deep inner joy of nonsexual bonding. The person who grows in the virtue of chastity—being pure in mind and body—learns to touch non-sexually and to have the deep and abiding human pleasure of nonsexual bonding, either with one's own sex or with the opposite sex, either with adults or with children. This is the warm affection St. Peter and St. Paul encourage among Christians (cf. Romans 12:10; Philippians 1:8; Philippians 2:1; and 2 Peter 1:7). Lust, however, precludes nonsexual bonding and relationships become sexualized.

Sex addiction is as obsessive-compulsive as any other addiction. Just as AA classifies alcoholism as a disease so did St. Augustine classify lust. Sixteen hundred years ago he noted: "Sinful lust is not nature, but a disease of nature."[90] There are some who do not understand this description of addiction as a disease, but it is not a new understanding, as we see from St. Augustine. The seven deadly sins are all diseases of the soul. Just as physical diseases destroy the body, so the seven deadly sins are lethal to soul and body.

Just as the few beers he began with no longer satisfy the alcoholic, so too with the lust addict: he increases his acting out. Masturbation is regarded by the secular world as harmless, yet in reality it turns a person in on himself, increasing his inability to bond non-sexually with others, including the spouse. C.S. Lewis gave the following response to a young man who asked him about masturbation:

For me the real evil of masturbation would be that it takes an appetite which, in lawful use, leads the individual out of himself to complete his own personality in that of another and turns it back; sends the man back into the prison of himself, there to keep a harem of brides. And this harem, once admitted, works against his ever getting out and really uniting with a real woman. For the harem is: always accessible, always subservient, calls for no sacrifices or adjustments, and can be endowed with erotic and psychological attractions which no real woman can rival. Among those shadowy brides he is: always adored, always the perfect love, no demand is made of his unselfishness, no mortification ever imposed on his vanity. In the end, they become merely the medium through which he increasingly adores himself.[91]

Sinful lust fosters escapism and the inability to relate to real people with physically imperfect bodies. What is the remedy? We need help from a Power greater than ourselves to overcome our sinful tendencies instead of indulging them. As with alcohol addiction, lust addiction is essentially a spiritual problem and calls for a spiritual solution. One can find that solution in twelve-step fellowship. One of the desert monks of the sixth century advises: "Do not think that you will overcome the demon of lust by entering into an argument with him. Wounded nature is on the devil's side and he has the best argument. So the person who decides to struggle against his flesh and to overcome it by his own efforts is fighting in vain. The truth is that unless the Lord overturns the house of the flesh and builds the house of the soul, the person who wishes to overcome it has watched and fasted in vain. Surrender by offering up to the Lord the weakness of your nature."[92] Help must be sought in a Power greater than oneself. God alone can overcome the demon of lust.

Jesus taught the Samaritan woman who, after five husbands, was in her sixth relationship, that her thirst was really for the living water and that "whoever drinks of the water that I shall give will never thirst" (John 4:14). It is the same for the Hugh Heffners of the world. In truth, they are hungry for the Infinite. Man's thirst is infinite and should lead him to God, who alone is infinite. The recovering lust addict learns to pray with St. Augustine, "Lord, help me to find in You what I was looking for in lust," for in reality, his thirst was a thirst for the living God who alone can satiate.

Pornographic Culture

As St. Thomas Aquinas explains, "We must not only revere God in Himself, but also that which is His in each one."[93] It is such a grave evil to participate in the abuse of God's image by the use of pornography, for all persons are His image and Christ warns, "Whatever you do to the least, I will count as done to me" (cf. 25:40). This should deter any serious Christian from indulging in and supporting the abuse of God's image with the pornography industry, or for the one already addicted to seriously seek help. Lust has infiltrated every aspect of American life, stripping sexuality of everything except mere physical excitement. And we are reaping the whirlwind. Sociologists Murray Straus and Larry Baron (University of New Hampshire) found that rape rates are highest in states that have high sales of sex magazines and lax enforcement of pornography laws.[94]

Porn is estimated to be a multibillion-dollar industry in America alone, banking at least ten times what it did in 1970, the first time the U.S. government evaluated the retail value of the nation's then-fledgling hardcore film, television, and retail market.[95] Prolonged exposure to pornography led Ted Bundy to rape and brutally murder an untold number of young women. The day before his execution on January 24, 1989, he granted psychologist James Dobson an exclusive interview, in which he speculated on the reasons for his heinous behavior and warned society against the addictive effects of pornography.[96]

Two extremes should always be avoided: condoning illicit attractions and condemning persons with those attractions. Christ never condones sin, but at the same time never condemns the sinner (as with the woman caught in adultery, for example, John 5:14).

Sexaholics Anonymous, S-Anon, and S-Ateen

In the late seventies, a group was born out of the experiences of people addicted to lust. The group became known as Sexaholics Anonymous (SA).[97] It is a growing international fellowship of men and women, with healing for spouses of the addict in S-Anon and for teenagers from families with lust addiction in S-Ateen. SA recognizes lust as an essentially spiritual problem calling for a spiritual solution. As stressed by Christ, healing comes to an individual when he gathers with others (cf. Matthew 18:20). It is in an anonymous fellowship such as SA that a person with lust addiction can learn from others who share with him their experience, strength, and hope.

Lust, Chastity, Prudishness, and Recovery

Recovery from the effects of sin in our lives should encompass all areas of our lives. It was this realization that led the spouses of AA to recognize how the disease of alcoholism affected them, and they began their own recovery in Alanon. Others recognized the obsessive-compulsive disorder in themselves, only their drug wasn't alcohol. It was food (and thus the birth of Overeaters Anonymous), lust (and the birth of Sexaholics Anonymous), emotional problems (Emotions Anonymous), codependency (Codependents Anonymous), compulsive working (Workaholics Anonymous), gambling (Gamblers Anonymous), drugs (Narcotics Anonymous), etc. In truth, the principles of the steps are gleaned from two thousand years of lived Christian experience and encompass true Christian living. They are principles of the spiritual life that should be lived by all Christians. Without them, a person's life becomes unmanageable and susceptible to addictive and codependent behavior. With this being said, one can understand the need for a fellowship of men and women who share their experience, strength, and hope with each other that they may solve their common problem and help others recover from lust addiction. In this regard it is no different from any other of the above addictions. As a fellowship SA has helped other lust addicts to recover.

Lust addiction is one of the most devastating addictions in contemporary society, given the large numbers of people who ruin their lives and careers with sexual behaviors they can no longer control. It has brought untold harm to innocent children, objectification to woman, and destruction to the Church's credibility. Lust, a serious disorder of nature, has become for many a mood-altering drug. As with alcoholism, it transcends personality, gender, and socio-economic status. It is found among men and women, clergy and laity, old and young. The symptoms of lust addiction are not unlike those for alcoholism: they include an obsession with sex that becomes more important than family, friends, and work. The addict often progresses to frequent destructive sexual encounters to feel normal, and their sexual mood-altering "experience" becomes central to their lives. The addict often confuses nurturing with sex. Fortunately there is a way out and many men and women have found that way in and through the SA fellowship. Through recovery in this twelve-step fellowship, where recovering members share their experiences, strength, and hope, a person is able to face his shame, love himself, and become clean and sober. For the married person this means that intimacy in marriage becomes good, clean, and free—as intended by God.

A Prayer to Guard Purity

Immaculate Virgin Mary, I confide my chastity to your maternal heart. I ask your help to guard my senses, especially the eyes, for an unchaste eye is the messenger of an unchaste heart. Knowing my pride, I pray for humility that invites the mercy of God. Knowing that I am wounded, I shall not be surprised at the urge of concupiscence, but trusting in your care, I rely on your protection and all the graces that I need from your divine Son to live a chaste life. Amen.

Conclusion

The Freedom to Love

> *I will walk about in freedom, for I
> have cherished your precepts.*
>
> Psalm 119:45

For centuries Christian culture has given us a moral sense of the deadliness of sin. Fourteenth century author Geoffrey Chaucer, in his *Canterbury Tales,* demonstrates that self-awareness is a pre-requisite for the pilgrim's journey to salvation. He ends his adventurous tome with the Parson's Tale, which is a sermon about the seven deadly sins and the need for repentance as the Christian makes his pilgrimage through life. Today's culture has happily thrown off the wisdom of the ages. For example, in August of 1993, MTV did a special titled, "Seven Deadly Sins: An MTV News Special Report," wherein various artists were interviewed on the topic. Responses showed that most of the deadly sins were viewed not as serious by artists such as Kirstie Alley, for example, who explained, "I don't think pride is a sin, and I think some idiot made that up. Who made that up anyway?" When told that it came from Christian thinkers like St. Thomas Aquinas, she retorted, "Not to knock monks or anything, but this anti-ego thing doesn't work for me." Aerosmith's Steven Tyler was equally smug, saying, "I live for lust." It's unfortunate that though there is plenty of contemporary evidence on the harm inflicted by the deadly sins, people refuse to acknowledge this because of their unwillingness to deny themselves their drugs.

The seven deadly sins are shown to have been destructive of the love of God. Pride, then envy, then anger are shown to be sins of ego-centricism that produce harm to oneself and others; sloth is the failure to allow love to direct the will to do good; avarice, greed, and lust are excessive love for things other than God. The sinfulness lies in loving the blessings of God more than God. A very real and profound moral disorder is found in unregenerate man. We all stand in need of grace if God's love is to become active in our lives and redemption our end. The person who abuses himself through addiction in truth does not love himself, and if a person does not love himself, he shall hate his neighbor as himself. The purpose of our vocation as Christians is to reveal God's love. Only when His love is revealed does life have meaning. It is an awesome vocation. There is nothing so beautiful as the revelation of God's love, which alone makes man fully alive. We can communicate this love only by His grace, which heals the wounds of sin and sets us free to love.

Dependency and Recovery

Bill Wilson, one of the founders of Alcoholics Anonymous, used the spirituality of the twelve steps to overcome his compulsive drinking, but he was left depressed much of the time and wondered if the steps could help with depression. For a long time he pondered over the prayer of Saint Francis:

> **Lord, make me an instrument of your peace.**
> **Where there is hatred, let me sow love;**
> **where there is injury, pardon;**
> **where there is doubt, faith;**
> **where there is despair, hope;**
> **where there is darkness, light;**
> **and where there is sadness, joy.**
>
> **O Divine Master, grant that I may not so much seek**
> **to be consoled as to console;**
> **to be understood as to understand;**
> **to be loved as to love.**
> **For it is in giving that we receive;**
> **it is in pardoning that we are pardoned;**
> **and it is in dying that we are born to eternal life.**

"Here is the formula," he thought, "but why doesn't it work?" Suddenly he realized what the matter was: his dependency. "My basic flaw had always been dependence—almost absolute dependence—on people or circumstances to supply me with the prestige, security and the like. Failing to get these according to my perfectionistic dreams and specifications, I had fought for them. And when defeat came, so did my depression. There wasn't a chance of making the outgoing love of St. Francis a workable and joyous way of life until these fatal and almost absolute dependencies were cut away..."[98] Bill learned that he couldn't avail himself of God's love until he was able to offer back to God by loving others as God wanted; but he couldn't love others as God would have him insofar as he was a victim to his dependencies. His dependency demanded the control of people and circumstances around him; failing to get these according to his specifications, he was left depressed. His problem was self; his solution: to love others regardless of the return to him, which was the challenge of the Prayer of St. Francis. In that way alone could he avail himself of God's love. He came to see that understanding comes only through love. That was the primary healing circuit. A willingness to love others without any expectations was the way to avail oneself of God's love. One commandment of love with a three-fold aspect: God, self, and others. Through the prayer of St. Francis, Bill came to realize that the love of God is learned through loving other people, and loving others entails detachment from sin and self. Sin involves a real and profound moral disorder that prevents us from loving as God would have us.

We have seen that the love Christ commands is not an emotional love as such. Nevertheless, as we grow in self-understanding and come to love ourselves as we are because of God's unmerited love for us, there will be some stirring of emotion, some warmth in the love of neighbor as grace begins to perfect our wounded nature. It is true that Christ commanded us to *love* everybody but gave us no command to *like* everybody; nonetheless, such an expression of Christian love is not cold and uncaring. As a person grows in virtue, his love becomes compassionate and caring, with heartfelt tenderness. Love, thus felt, adds something rich to our care for others, even our enemies. Such was the compassionate love of Christ. From the cross could be heard love's plea, "Father, forgive them for they know not what they do" (Luke 23:34).

Selfless Love

This kind of love is something the world knows little or nothing about. When it was revealed that Mother Teresa spent most of her life in spiritual darkness, the response of many was that she was a fake. Take for example the response given in *Newsweek* by atheist Christopher Hitchens. He remarked that the revelation of her darkness gave evidence that Mother Teresa was "a confused old lady who...had for all practical purposes ceased to believe..." Her darkness, Hitchens says, gives evidence that God was absent from her life.[99] Imagine that: merely a confused old lady, and yet one without whose compassionate love over 90,000 lepers would still remain in the gutters of the world's cities, for there are no atheist leper colonies!

In truth, Mother Teresa's desire was to imitate the sacrificial and true love of her Spouse. Why would Christ, the Son of God, allow Himself to be spit on, mocked, and crucified? God humbled Himself out of love for sinful man, and still man is arrogant. True love—God's love—is selfless and humble, and so it became for the humble Mother Teresa. There was no consolation for her from heaven and none from earth. The darkness of faith was her light. St. Bernard uses the image of a boiling pot to explain how God is at work in the soul despite the dark night of faith. As long as fire burns beneath the pot, the water within bubbles with life. So also, if a person's life is full of goodness, bubbling over with the theological virtues of faith, hope, and love, together with the moral virtues that they engender, it is certain that the divine fire burns within. Mother Teresa was full of tender love for the poorest of the poor and spent herself in their service, even in the midst of the deepest darkness. One time when I was in the Missionary of Charity home for the dying in Calcutta, a Hindu man, who offered his service to help the poor, remarked to me, "Father, I have to come at least once a week to get my fix." He told how it made him feel so good to help out at the home for the dying. In Calcutta, Mother Teresa took away some people's fear of the poor and untouchables. This Hindu man's free service to the poor was a good thing, but it was not Christian as such. To come and offer one's service when it *doesn't* feel good, indeed, when it feels painful and dark—that's the love of Christ at work in a soul. Such was the case with Mother Teresa. There was nothing in it for her but darkness, and she loved Him anyway in imitation of His love for her. This is the love that saves souls and changes the world for the better, the love for which we engage in the spiritual battle against the seven deadly sins. It is the path to heaven. The darkness of Mother Teresa's spiritual life was the darkness of disinterested love, the power of which dispels all evil, washes guilt away, restores lost innocence, and brings mourners joy; it casts out hatred, brings us peace, and humbles earthly pride—something the unconverted Christopher Hitchenses of the world cannot comprehend.

We can say, with the words of St. Peter, that we must make every effort to support our recovery from the effects of sin "with virtue, and virtue with knowledge, knowledge with self-control, self-control with endurance, endurance with devotion, and devotion with mutual affection, mutual affection with love" (2 Peter 1: 5–7). All of Christian tradition fosters the virtues for the principle reason that they work. Only the virtuous are free to love. There is no salvation without love and we only have this life to increase our capacity for love. Indulging the seven deadly sins kills our ability to love as God deserves to be loved. Indeed, as Pope Benedict remarks, "If man's heart is not good, then nothing else can turn out good."[100] Sin darkens the culture because it demeans human beings.

The law given by God is given for the advancement of a civilization of love. Every element of the law of God makes for health and wholeness, while its contravention makes for the spiritual disease and deformation of the human person. In obeying the moral law, man cooperates with God in giving birth to His kingdom of love. The Christian is called by Christ to live his moral life in the light of faith, and this faith reveals to him the primacy of love, correctly understood. "Whatever is true, whatever is honorable, whatever is just, whatever is pure, whatever is lovely, whatever is gracious, if there is any excellence, if there is anything worthy of praise, think about these things" (Philippians 4:8).

We are called to a life of freedom that begins when we acquire the virtues. Putting the principles of the twelve steps into practice involves a struggle because they run counter to the demands of our wounded nature. The struggle is one of exercising the virtues. "A virtue is an habitual and firm disposition to do the good. It allows the person not only to perform good acts, but to give the best of himself. The virtuous person tends toward the good with all his sensory and spiritual powers; he pursues the good and chooses it in concrete actions.[101] The goal of a virtuous life is to be restored to the image and likeness of God in which we were created. With regard to the image of God in man, Pope Benedict remarks, "The vocation of love is what makes the person an authentic image of God; one becomes similar to God to the degree that one becomes one who loves." Without taking the moral life radically seriously, there can be no hope of genuine recovery because, ultimately, we are recovering from the effects of sin in our lives, sin conducive to addiction and codependency.

As we have shown, the seven deadly sinful inclinations of our wounded nature bring forth a host of ineffectual and sinful behavior. From pride come presumption, ambition, boasting, hypocrisy, argumentativeness, and disobedience to the dictates of truth. From envy, hatred, detraction, calumny, gossip, joy at another's misfortune and sadness at his success. From anger, quarreling, boldness, pugnacity, cursing, indignation, and blasphemy. From sloth, timidity, bitterness, despair, affected ignorance, and undue curiosity about dangerous things. From gluttony proceed overindulgence, drunkenness, and vulgarity. From avarice, hardheartedness, anxiety for worldly things, injustice, deceit, fraud, greed, and perjury. From lust, mental blindness, inconsideration, inconstancy, worldliness, harassment, pornographic behavior, and the incapacity for intimacy. These are the ills that prevent our responding in a reasonable, responsible, and loving way to the troubles of life.

The Civilizing Effect of Love

When I first went to Calcutta, there was a serious car accident, and the people standing around, who appeared to be very gentle, grabbed ahold of the driver who caused the accident, dragged him out of this car, and plucked out his eyes. I remained ever horrified and afraid each time I had to venture out with a driver. When I told this to a fellow friar, he sent me a Web notice where some men in a strict Muslim country had recently had their eyes gouged out for some crime or other. In my room is a framed picture of a beautiful young woman holding a dish with her two eyes: St. Lucy. St. Lucy had her eyes plucked out for refusing to surrender her Christian faith. I was horrified to find out that it is still a practice today. As I reflected on it and read about it, I realized that the practice was done away with in Christian countries, much in the same way a rape became a crime for the first time under the law when the Roman Empire became Christian. It is evident that the Christian Gospel has tamed the savagery of the human heart in every place where its roots went deep. With the loss of the Christian faith in the West, this savagery is returning. If we love what we have received from the life-giving Gospel given by Christ, we should meditate on these blessings and be willing to root out from our lives the seven deadly sins and their offspring.

Because of the Gospel, Christians have rescued the unwanted of the world. Years ago in a large capital of a poor nation, while working with Mother Teresa's nuns, I met a little girl they had rescued from abandonment. The girl was blind and had only one hand. After being with the sisters for a while, an American couple adopted her. Recently on *The X Factor* in Australia, a young man from Iraq was featured. Conceived by a woman who had been exposed to chemical warfare, two brothers were born without limbs and discarded. Mother Teresa's Missionaries of Charity found them in a box and brought them home to their orphanage. An Irish Catholic woman adopted them and brought them home to Australia.[102] Likewise the actor Jim Caviezel and his wife Kerri, unable to have children of their own, have adopted handicapped children. This is the inspiring heritage of Christian civilization. Until the coming of Christ, the unwanted had no worth and no home. Seeing such inspiring witnesses of hope should encourage all of us who follow Christ to root out the seven deadly sins from our lives so that the Good News about the unchanging God of love can continue to be preached and accepted.

Whereas the seven deadly sins are no more than sad efforts to satiate the thirst for love, Gospel faith shows us the way to true love's fulfillment. Faith is not an intellectual assent purely and simply to a set of dogmas. It is a way of being, the way taught by Christ. If a Christian is not interested in spreading the Gospel through love, his salvation is at risk. He should fear it will go worse for him on judgment day than those brought up in strict Islamic cultures where love of enemies is not promulgated. Christian life entails the morality of virtue, for virtue is a necessary condition for submission to the truth. Moral laws, like physical laws, tell us how to handle ourselves harmoniously with reality. The command to love would not be possible without those moral laws. They deepen the capacity of the human heart to face all troubles with hope and train us in genuine love. And only with love are the doors of life opened wide to salvation. Only by rooting out the seven deadly sins and acquiring the virtues are we free to love.

End Notes

1. Robert Moynihan, ed., *Let God's Light Shine Forth: The Spiritual Vision of Pope Benedict XVI*, (Image Books, 2006), p. 165.

2. http://oas.samhsa.gov/

3. http://www.nida.nih.gov

4. For example, a man is jailed for having molested his step-daughters—and rightly so. But in getting out of prison, he has to attend therapy sessions wherein he is counseled to masturbate while fantasizing about some girl he was attracted to. Fortunately, the Catholic Bishop got involved and the court allowed the man to attend Sexaholics Anonymous, whose definition of sexual sobriety is thoroughly Christian, i.e. reasonable. Without any ties to traditional morality, psychologists are having to reinvent the wheel, often with grave consequences. See footnote # 89.

5. *Twelve-steps and Twelve Traditions* (New York: AA World Services, Inc., 1965), p. 42ff.

6. By "Judeo-Christian" I mean that tradition that finds its roots in the moral world of the Hebrew Bible, from which both Judaism and Christianity emerged.

7. See, for example, the influence of Episcopal priest Samuel Shoemaker in *Courage to Change: The Christian Roots of the Twelve-Step Movement*, compiled and edited by Bill Pittman and Dick B. (Center City: Hazelden; 1994). Bill Wilson said the following in an address at the St. Louis AA convention in 1955: "It was from Sam Shoemaker, that we absorbed most of the Twelve-steps of Alcoholics Anonymous, steps that express the heart of AA's way of life. Dr. Silkworth gave us the needed knowledge of our illness, but Sam Shoemaker had given us the concrete knowledge of what we could do about it, he passed on the spiritual keys by which we were liberated. The early AA got its ideas of self-examination, acknowledgement of character defects, restitution for harm done, and working with others straight from the Oxford Group and directly from Sam Shoemaker, their former leader in America, and from nowhere else." Another priestly influence on Bill was the Jesuit priest Fr. Ed Dowling. After his death, Bill said of him (referring to Fr. Ed's last article for AA's *Grapevine)*, "Father Ed, an early and wonderful friend of AA, died as this last message went to press. He was the greatest and most gentle soul to walk this planet. I was closer to him than to any other human being on earth." On the relationship of Fr. Dowling and Bill see *The Soul of Sponsorship:*

*The Friendship of Fr. Ed Dowling, S.J. and Bill Wilson
in* Letters, by Robert Fitzgerald, S.J. (Center City:
Hazelden, 1995). For the influence of Sister Ignatia on
AA, see *Sister Ignatia: The Angel of Alcoholics Anonymous*
by Mary Darrah (Chicago: Loyola University Press;
1992). For AA's touching tribute to Sister Ignatia at
the time of her death, see silkworth.net.

8. To note a few examples, John Adams, second president
    of the United States and signer of the Declaration
    of Independence, notes that "Our Constitution was
    made only for a moral and religious people. It is wholly
    inadequate to the government of any other." To this
    we can add the thoughts of our first president, George
    Washington, who wrote, "Let us with caution indulge
    the supposition that morality can be maintained
    without religion. Reason and experience both forbid us
    to expect that national morality can prevail in exclusion
    of religious principle." And Alexander Hamilton, "In all
    those dispositions which promote political happiness,
    religion and morality are essential props. In vain does he
    claim the praise of patriotism, who labors to subvert or
    undermine these great pillars of human happiness, these
    firmest foundations of the duties of men and citizens.
    The mere politician, equally with the pious man, ought
    to respect and cherish them." And Samuel Adams,
    "A general dissolution of principles and manners will
    more surely overthrow the liberties of America than the
    whole force of the common enemy. While the people
    are virtuous they cannot be subdued; but when once

they lose their virtue then will be ready to surrender their liberties to the first external or internal invader."

9. The pronoun "he" in this book is meant in its inclusive sense. Not all agree on "he" being inclusive, but human experience, in my opinion, shows it indeed to be inclusive, in the following sense. Women who take upon themselves occupations traditionally male, like firemen or policemen, do so in a masculine way (they dress like men, wear men's clothes and shoes, etc.), whereas men who take upon themselves traditionally female occupations do so—not in a feminine way—but in a masculine way, like male nurses. Likewise, actresses being interviewed most often refer to themselves as "actors." But I've never heard a male star refer to himself as an "actress," for the obvious reason that "actress" is exclusive, as is the pronoun "she."

10. All biblical quotations are from the New American Bible, Revised Edition (Charlotte: St. Benedict Press, 2011).

11. http://www.addiction-treatment-centers.com/ addiction-articles/addiction-impact-on-the-family

12. Born into a Jewish family in Austria, Frankl excelled as a doctor, specializing in neurology and psychiatry. In 1942, along with his wife and his parents, he was deported to a concentration camp. See his study, *Man's Search for Meaning* (Boston: Beacon Press, 1963). Between 1942 and 1945 Frankl labored in four different camps, including Auschwitz, while his parents, brother,

and pregnant wife perished.

13. Robert Leslie, *Jesus and Logotheraphy* (Abingdon Press, 1965), p. 18.

14. For example, Dr. Bernard Nathanson relates how he inflated statistics in order to promote his agenda when founding the National Abortion Rights League. See his *The Hand of God: Journey from Death to Life* (Lewiston, N.Y.: Life Cycle Books; 1996).

15. Thomas Aquinas, *Summa Theologiæ* (henceforth *ST*), III, Q. 16; trans. Fathers of the English Dominican Province (New York: Benziger Bros. 1948); cf. Ephesians 4:11–13.

16. Austin Flannery, *The Documents of Vatican II* (Costello Pub. Co., 1975), *GS* 13 § 1.

17. *Catechism of the Catholic Church* (Doubleday, 2003). Henceforth rendered *CCC*.

18. Augustine, *Of True Religion*, in *Augustine: Earlier Writings*, ed. and trans. John H. S. Burleigh (Philadelphia and London, 1953), xxxviii, 69, p. 260.

19. For what follows see *Self-Knowledge and Self-Discipline: How to Know and Govern Yourself* by Basil Maturin; St. Anthony Guild Press, Paterson, New Jersey, 1939, pp. 69ff.

20. Note the title of George Stephanopoulos' book on Clinton, *All Too Human*, (Back Bay Books, 2000) as if it were human to sexually abuse women!

21. You can read about this case in Olivia McFadden's biography of Marcus' sister, *Greater Love Than This* (Xlibris Corp., 2004).

22. See, for example, Galatians 5:16-26, Ephesians 4:31-5:2; 2 Timothy 3:1-3:9; 1 Peter 2:1-2:3.

23. cf. *CCC* #1866

24. St. Augustine, *Confessions,* I, 1. (Penguin Classics, 1961).

25. Hans Urs Von Balthasar, *The Glory of the Lord: A Theological Aesthetics.* Volume VII: *Theology: The New Covenant,* (San Francisco: Ignatius Press, 1989), p. 83.

26. Augustine, *City of God,* 15.22, (Cambridge University Press, 1998).

27. Pope Benedict XVI, *Introduction to Christianity* (San Francisco: Ignatius Press, 2004), p. 306.

28. cf. Mother Teresa, *Love: A Fruit Always in Season* (San Francisco: Ignatius Press, 1987).

29. Alice von Hildebrand, cited at *InsideCatholic.com,* July 1, 2007.

30. Augustine, *City of God,* 14.6.

31. Epictetus, cited by Sharon Lebell in *Art of Living: The Classical Manual on Virtue, Happiness, and Effectiveness* (San Francisco: Harper, 1995).

32. See the recent study of Art and Larraine Bennett for an introduction to the role of the passions, *The Emotions*

God Gave You: A Guide for Catholics to Healthy and Holy Living (The Word Among Us Press, 2011).

33. As a person who grew up in a family with addiction and mental illness—and therefore has learned of the need for effective healing and feeling of the emotions—I recommend further study of this important subject. In addition to the above-mentioned work by the Bennetts, see also Conrad Baars, *Feeling and Healing Your Emotions* (Logos International, 1979).

34. ST II-II, Q. 92 Art. 1.

35. All emotions are feelings but not all feelings are emotions. I feel hungry is not an emotion. An emotion has a psychic element to it.

36. Catholic News Service article by Cindy Wilson, "Pope Benedict says traditional family must be defended." June 7, 2005.

37. Augustine, *On Free Choice of the Will* (see I.15 and II.13); trans. Thomas Williams. (Indianapolis: Hackett Pub. Co. 1993).

38. On evil as a privation, cf. St. Thomas Aquinas, *Summa Contra Gentiles*, III, 7–9; *ST*, I, Q. 48. Art. I. (Indiana: University of Notre Dame Press, 1991).

39. We see this in St. Thomas's explanation (*ST*, II-II, Q. 153, Art. 4): "a capital vice is that which has an exceedingly desirable end so that in his desire for it

a man goes on to the commission of many sins all of which are said to originate in that vice as their chief source."

40. For this reason Aquinas only uses the term "vices."

41. This list of seven capital virtues originates in an epic poem written by an early Christian poet, Aurelius Prudentius Clemens, at the end of the fourth century. The poem, *Psychomachia* (The Soul's Battle), is an allegory that describes seven virtues warring again the seven vices.

42. *ST* I-II, Q. 64

43. Strictly speaking, and for St. Thomas, abstinence, chastity, and sobriety fall under temperance.

44. The author's word for frigidity.

45. Thomas Dubay *Evidential Power of Beauty*, (San Francisco: Ignatius Press, 1999) p. 252.

46. Augustine, *The Morals of the Catholic Church*, 15.25 (Whitefish, MT: Kessinger Publications, 2005).

47. *ST* II-II, Q. 161, Art. 1, ad. 3.

48. John Paul II, *Redemptor Hominis*, (Slough: Society of St. Paul, 1979).

49. *ST* II-II, Q. 25, Art. 4, ad. 3.

50. Decree on Original Sin, Council of Trent, (DS 1511).

51. *Benedict XVI, Pope, Commentary on Philippians 2:6–11 "The Paradoxical Emptying of the Divine Word," General audience delivered in Rome, (Zenit.org, June 1, 2005), n. 1.*

52. *Maxims and Counsels* #24 in *The Collected Works of St. John of the Cross*, trans. by Kieran Kavanaugh, O.C.D. (Washington, D.C.: ICS Publications, p. 675).

53. Quoted by Thomas Merton in *Wisdom of the Desert* (New York: New Directions, 1970), p. 83

54. C.S. Lewis, "Christianity and Culture," in *Christian Reflection,* ed. W. Hooper Grand Rapids: Eerdmans, 1967), p. 14

55. *ST* II-II, Q. 161, Art. 5, ad, 2

56. Saint Teresa of Avila, *The Way of Perfection*, (New York: Image Books), chapter 39:1–2, p. 256.

57. Olivier Clément, *The Roots of Christian Mysticism* (New York: New City Press, 1995), p. 154. Mentioned also by St. Thomas in his discussion on humility, *ST* Q. 161, Art. 5, a. 1.

58. From the website www.benedictinesofheartshermitage. org.

59. *ST* II-II, Q. 161, Art. 4.

60. See, for example, *ST* I-II Q. 77, Art. 4, ad 4.

61. This could also be said of social animals, like monkeys. As Dr. Maté notes, "…conditions in the laboratory

powerfully influence which animals will succumb to addiction. Among monkeys, for example, subordinate males who are stressed and relatively isolated are the ones more likely to self-administer cocaine." *In the Realm of Hungry Ghosts*, (Berkeley: North Atlantic Books, 2010), pp. 144–145.

62. See, for example, the booklet by the National Alliance on Mental Health *Mental Health Crisis Planning.*

63. John E. Douglas and Mark Olshaker, *Obsession* (Pocket, 1995) p. 71. See also John Douglas, *Mind Hunter: Inside the FBI's Elite Serial Crime Unit* (Scribner, 1995).

64. Candace Snow and David Willard, *I'm Dying to Take Care of You; Nurses and Codependence*, (Professional Counselor Books, 1989).

65. For what follows, see the interview with Dr. Nathanson, www.childrenofthecode.org. See also his *Shame and Pride: Affect, Sex, and the Birth of the Self* (New York: Norton, 1992).

66. ibid.

67. *ST* II-II, Q. 36, Art. 3.

68. *ST* I-II, Q. 63, Art. 2, ad 1.

69. See, for example, the entry on envy in *The Stanford Encyclopedia of Philosophy.*

70. *The New York Times*, Tuesday, November 22, 2011.

71. *Associated Press* news report July 7, 2008.

72. Cf. University of Arizona Study at www. foodproductdaily.com'

73. Bob Anderson, "Debt, greed, and human avarice," March 29 column in *The Wenathee World.*

74. *ST*, II-II, Q. 158, Art. 1

75. For the above, see *ST* II-II, Q. 158.

76. *ST* I-II, Q. 25, Art. 3, ad. 3

77. St. John Chrysostom, *Homilies on the Gospel of St. Matthew*, 30, 5 (Whitefish, MT: Kessinger Pub. Co., 2010).

78. Aristotle, *Nicomachean Ethics*, Book 4, chap. 5.

79. *ST* II–II, Q. 157, Art. 3.

80. This is a word I have coined after many years of usage and have asked the editor to leave it in.

81. Augustine, *Letter 138*, Chapter 2, 11.

82. Augustine, *The Lord's Sermon*, 75, 66.

83. Caleb Carr, *The Alienist* (New York: Random House, 1994), p.198.

84. New York Times article, "Obesity Rates Hit Plateau in U.S., Data Suggest" by Pam Belluck, January 13, 2010.

85. *ST* II-II Q. 146 a. 1.

86. *ST* II-II Q. 148 a. 1.

87. cf *ST* Q. 148

88. Augustine, Sermon 210

89. *ST* II-II Q. 142, Art. 1.

90. Cited in *Seven Short Treatises of St. Augustine* trans. John Henry Parker, (Whitefish, MT; Kessinger Pub. Co, 2007), p. 258.

91. *Letter (March 6, 1956) from C.S. Lewis to a Mr. Masson,* Wade Collection, Wheaton College, Wheaton, IL; cited in Leanne Payne, *The Broken Image* (Grand Rapids: Baker Books, 1995).

92. John Climacus, *The Ladder of Divine Ascent* (Boston: Holy Transfiguration Monastery, 1978).

93. *ST* II-II, Q. 161, Art. 3, ad 1.

94. "Legitimate Violence, Violent Attitudes, and Rape: A Test of the Cultural Spillover Theory," *Annals of the New York Academy of Science,* Vol. 528: 79–110, 1985.

95. From CNN website.

96. From the magazine *Love One Another,* Number 19, article titled "Stop Pornography" by Sister Maria Dwiek, S.J.K.

97. See www.sa.org and www.sanon.org.

98. Bill Wilson, *The Language of the Heart* (New York: AA Grapevine, 1988), p. 236.

99. *Newsweek* August 28, 2007. "Teresa, Bright and Dark," by Christopher Hitchens. Such attitudes about a good and holy woman make it understandable how God could become man out of love and yet be put to death.

100. Pope Benedict XVI, *Jesus of Nazareth*, (New York: Doubleday, 2007), p. 33.

101. *CCC* #1803

102. For an inspiring look into their lives, search "Emmanuel Kelly" on Youtube.com. See also a similar and true story made into a movie with Cloris Leachman, *The Woman Who Willed a Miracle*.

CPSIA information can be obtained at www.ICGtesting.com
Printed in the USA
BVOW061222130512

289746BV00001B/4/P